A VIEW FROM THE FLOOR

A STROKE OF INSIGHT IN COSTA RICA

BY RILEY JACKSON

A Tigress Publishing Book

ISBN: 978-1-59404-040-5
Library of Congress Control Number: 2010939125
Printed in the United States of America

Book Design & Illustrations: Steve Montiglio
Editor: Peter Atkins
Author Photo: S. Younger

10 9 8 7 6 5 4 3 2 1

All rights reserved. No part of this book may be transmitted in any form or by any means, electronically or mechanically including photocopying, recording or by any information storage or retrieval system without the written permission of the publisher except where permitted by law.

Requests for such permission should be submitted to:
Tigress Publishing
4831 Fauntleroy Way SW #103
Seattle, WA 98116

Copyright 2010 Riley Jackson

This is a work of fiction. All names, characters and incidents are either the product of the author's imagination or are used fictitiously. Any resemblance to actual persons, living or dead, business establishments, or other events or locals is entirely coincidental.

This book is dedicated to the therapists, doctors and nurses of the Veterans Administration Seattle Medical Center who put up with my childish antics, paranoia, and general poor behavior while in their care. I literally owe them my present life. To say I will never forget you is inadequate. May you all lead full and healthy lives.

The names of the characters here have been changed to protect those few innocent souls as well as the many guilty ones.

I was confused.

Something bad had happened, and something worse was coming.

For some reason my thinking was slow, and my eyes were having difficulty in bringing whatever was approaching me into focus. It appeared to be a dirty brown blob, about four feet wide, and slowly making its way toward my face. I had no doubt that it was coming to kill me.

I had to blink several times before I could get my eyes to begin focusing but, as my angel of death moved closer, I was finally able to see it more clearly.

As it came into focus, its size diminished but other elements became clearer. My would-be executioner had brown wispy rabbit-ear antennas sticking out of an ugly and deformed head, the antenna ears moving back and forth and obviously trying to locate my hiding place. Its intent toward me was clear, and very unpleasant.

Through my befuddlement and confusion, my damaged brain finally managed to see just what exactly this monster was. The thing heading my way was nothing more than a cockroach.

I shouldn't have been surprised. Just like in that Julie Andrews movie, the hills of Costa Rica are alive. Not with the sound of music, but the sound of copulating cockroaches.

Long ago I had managed to overcome my disgust and the association with filth that these creatures conjured up. If I hadn't, I couldn't have stayed long in this beautiful land. Cockroaches, when provided with the right environment (and the whole country of Costa

Rica is the right environment), can grow to impressive sizes, especially when you're semiconscious and viewing one from several inches away.

It was no wonder that my damaged brain felt the advancing insect was going to kill me. It would only be taking a karmic revenge for the many members of his or her extended family I had dispatched. From a cockroach perspective, I fit the profile of a serial killer.

My cockroach victims numbered in the hundreds, if not thousands. As a new resident in Costa Rica my first kill was filled with the feeling of anxiety, the thrill of success, and the smell of my victim's guts after I opened it up with a flat blade shovel. Usually those I targeted died quickly, although I must admit I sometimes found inventive and deliciously long ways to snuff out their miserable lives. I have even boiled a few victims in hot water. The most satisfying of all was to pick them up and place them in the way of the army ants who regularly tried to invade my home.

But at the moment, all my cockroach-killing skills seemed to be beyond me; try as I might, I could not even move my arm to brush it away. So I decided to try something new. I decided to stop it with my morning breath.

It was early morning and I had not yet brushed my teeth. My mouth tasted like the bottom of a parrot's cage and my breath must have smelled worse. I figured that should do the trick. My eyesight, so slow to focus, must have affected my mouth, because that wasn't working either. I couldn't pucker up my lips to blow my breath. I had to settle for exhaling as hard as I could. I waited until the ugly beast was a couple of inches from my face and then exhaled as hard as I could.

Morning breath mightn't be much of a weapon but it was the only one at my disposal. And it must have been enough, because my would-be assassin altered his slow motion charge and headed off into the darker regions under the sink.

Which still left the question of what the hell had happened to me.

I don't know how long I had been lying there. All I knew was that something was not right. I felt no pain, but my body no longer worked. My left arm and leg had no feeling; they were still there but did not respond to any of my normal impulses to move them. My thoughts seemed to be lazy in coming, sort of like the slowed down process when I was drunk. After some mental chewing on this possibility, I was forced to conclude that I was neither drunk nor hung-over. Drunk was a goofy fun feeling, and so far there was no fun involved in my present state. There was however an encompassing feeling of peace, love and contentment due either to the excessive serotonin uptake inhibitors I was taking to keep me calm, or to the new condition into which I had just entered. Hangovers hurt and I was feeling no pain, so this was no hangover. What the hell was going on?

This whole weird journey started with swallowing water down the wrong pipe. Every morning, in an attempt to prolong my life, I took pills to lower my blood pressure, calm my nerves and generally help my sixty-one year old, balding, overweight and out of shape body survive another day. This particular morning the old body apparently wasn't up to par in the swallowing department and had screwed up the process. I'd taken a handful of my morning pills, including the aspirin the doctors had said would protect me from a fatal heart attack, and thrown them all into my mouth followed by a large gulp of water. I started coughing violently, almost retching in fact. I was worried that I might vomit.

I was standing at the kitchen sink, where the windows above it provided a view of the sun coming up over the coffee green mountains and the bamboo along the drive moving gently in the morning breeze. Convinced that the violent coughing was going to make me throw up, I leaned over the sink, believing that that was the best place for a morning hurl. It was a close call, but I successfully resisted the disagreeable urge to vomit. Which was the good news. The bad news was that I found I couldn't lift myself off the counter. I'd come to understand later that the problem was with my left hand but, in the moment, I was too confused to know that. All I knew was that there was something very wrong.

Strangely, I didn't feel any degree of panic. Instead, I was simply confused. I realized that I was thinking alright, so my mind must be okay. I knew what drunk was like, and this was definitely not drunk. Very slowly—and still without panic—I came to the understanding that my body wasn't working properly and that even if I could get myself away from the counter I'd probably fall down and maybe break something or crack my skull on the terrazzo floor. This was my first taste of getting no response when I tried to get my body to make normal movements. Maybe this was drunk after all, some new kind of drunk. Again, no panic. Just bewilderment, along with a calming feeling of peace and overwhelming love.

After several frustrating attempts to lower myself to the floor, I managed to do so using only my right arm. This unnatural action caused me to wedge my bulk under the kitchen sink where I promptly fell asleep, something I would do quite often during the next several days. Technically, I guess, I kept passing out. To me, though, it was just sleep. I was more tired than I could ever remember being. In addition, I felt that sleeping was a safe place to be.

The first time I regained consciousness was when I met my antenna-ladened cockroach friend. I was very relaxed, like I'd just woken from a peaceful night's sleep, and the floor under the kitchen sink was cool and pleasant against my cheek, a relief from the warmth of the early morning.

I needed to extricate myself from the clutches of that space under the sink where all sorts of foul and fragrant chemicals coexist with damp musky cloths and sponges in forced couplings. I struggled awkwardly, rolling this way and that, using my right arm and leg to move in the direction I wanted whenever my rolling put my arm and leg under me. It was a sort of uncoordinated crawl, but it at least eventually got me out from under the sink.

I was exhausted, and lay on the floor enjoying the coolness of the polished terrazzo against my cheek, a pleasant contrast to my too warm body. I remember consciously thinking that I was tired and that it was so pleasant just where I was that I might as well stay there and take another much needed nap. Which I promptly did.

When the next conscious thought registered, I was still there. I was so relaxed that I was drooling, the saliva wetting my cheek. Also I was quite comfortably peeing in my pants. It wasn't conscious, it was just happening. I could feel what was going on but had no control over it. I knew that peeing in one's pants was a no-no, but it really didn't matter to me in that moment. Peeing in one's pants had been freed from any social implications. I laughed as I remembered an old joke we used to say when I worked at a bank: "Doing a good job at the bank is like peeing in your best dark blue wool suit. It gives you a nice warm feeling but no one notices."

I stopped laughing when I realized that I was also pooping in my pants. It was then, I think, that it finally registered somewhere in the dark recesses of my dysfunctional mind that I might be in deep trouble. Peeing I could handle but loading my pants somehow crossed a more sensitive boundary. You could hide pee, but poop smelled and everyone would know.

We come into this world in a puddle of pee, I thought. *Maybe we go out the same way.* The thought that I could be leaving this earth evoked neither fear nor a review of my life. No white lights or voices, just the non-alarming and slowly developing thought that I might be going through the preliminary stages of dying. I remember thinking, *so this is what it's like*. Almost as if I would be given a test at some later date, so it was important to observe what was going on. The idea of death was in the abstract, sort of being there and not being there. It was happening to me but I wasn't me, I wasn't really part of what was going on.

Oddly, along with this acknowledgment of possible death came a warm secure conviction that I was not going to die. It might just have been the results of the tranquilizers I had taken when this whole episode started, but it felt like what was happening was supposed to happen and that it was no threat to my life. All I needed to do was roll with the punches and learn to contend with a new set of difficulties.

There were two entities involved with what was going on. One was me, my body and those thoughts. Then there was another me, existing around and in the body but somehow different from the other existence. This second me felt much larger than the physical me. I was curious and fascinated by this whole levels-of-existence thing and tried my best to understand the idea. But it's hard to pay attention when you keep passing out.

I figured that as long as I was so tired, I might as well go to bed. The bedroom was a good twenty-five feet away. It took forever to get my body to crawl into the bedroom using only my right arm and right leg, dragging the left arm and leg as dead weight. Like the old golf joke, "Hit the ball, drag Harry." I made it but, once there, I couldn't get into bed.

I heard Joel (pronounced Ho-el) chopping wood for his cooking fire. Joel was my seventy-four year old watchman who lived in a one room house on the farm. His job was to watch people stealing from me. He wouldn't *stop* them—Costa Ricans by nature do not engage in conflict—but he'd happily tell the Police who'd done it. I finally managed to yell loud enough to get his attention. He was unable to lift my 275 pound body into my bed. Fortunately my neighbor was working on the farm above mine that day and was able to assist Joel with putting me to bed, where I went blissfully back to sleep while soiling my pants.

My next recollection was a rather strange one. I was outside my body watching the unfolding drama. A drama that somehow I knew was not a danger to me in my present stroke induced state of being in peace and warmth. It could have been a memory of being in my mother's womb.

Now we were getting somewhere with this dying stuff. I was having an actual out of body experience, even though there was still no white light and not even one small angel. I was outside the front door, but not standing on the ground. I was floating at rooftop level, engulfed in warmth and peace. The peace I felt wasn't the peace that we normally think of, but one of overwhelming love. It was almost as if I knew it was my soul that was now in charge of what was going on. I'd read about people at these terminal stages of life meeting up with all those that had harmed them in the mortal life and forgiving them. That wasn't happening to me, even though the overwhelming feeling of love I was experiencing would have let me forgive all of the cockroaches that were infecting my food while I floated outside the front door. I wasn't in charge. My soul was. A greater, more powerful, expansion of soul.

I felt that this soul power was universal, more than just me. As such, there was nothing to be afraid of. In fact, at this point in my journey, fear never really entered into the equation. It would show up later in this emerging adventure but, at that moment, all I knew was that whatever was happening was supposed to be happening. Almost as if it was pre-planned or was a bigger part of me. Not the physical me, but Me, the BIG ME. That part of us that we all are aware of but really don't acknowledge as we go about moving our physical self through the physical life in which we find ourselves.

I saw my friend and taxi driver José arrive in his four wheel drive red taxi, followed closely by an old Toyota diesel powered jeep that served as the local ambulance. The jeep had an extended back end made of sheet metal into which patients—or bodies—were thrown. Along with the ambulance came my gringo friend James. He was in the cab crushing the driver and the driver's helper with his bulk. He looked to be a prime contender for the next stroke in town. He is a Friar Tuck looking individual who has been my companion on many precarious demented journeys. Most undertaken while completely bombed.

My neighbor had tried to use my CB radio to call

for help. Unfortunately turning it on and pressing the transmit button on the mic had proven beyond his mental abilities. So he had walked the four kilometers down the mountain into town where he notified my friend José the taxi driver that the gringo was not acting normal. Everyone arrived at once.

As I observed, from my floating position, the unfolding drama for those who had just arrived, I not only heard what they were saying but somehow felt the emotions they were feeling as they rushed to save my physical body. José appeared to be the one who felt the most concerned—at least that's what I was getting as I floated there in blissful love—while the gringo James felt only fear that he might screw up or that I was already dead. His vibrations were more socially oriented than José's. José's were more accepting of the bigger picture. To my perception, José's being was infinitely larger than the gringo's. I do not know why this was, it simply was.

Recalling this event now brings back all the feeling of well-being in the presence of love that I felt during the episode. I am blessed because of that expansion of being I felt and can still remember. I am blessed by the event and cursed with the inability to explain it in words. It transcends words. Or at least all the words that I know.

I do know that I can now relive the emotion and expansion of myself that was there when I was floating. I can do this whenever I take the time to step out of the physical world and acknowledge this other more real existence. This is my present legacy.

As I watched the ensuing Costa Rican fire drill, everyone concerned for me demonstrated their concern, either social or spiritual, by simultaneously giving orders to those in attendance while remaining deaf to orders directed towards them. When the ambulance attendants pulled the stretcher out of the ambulance, I was instantly back in my body inside the house, awake in my bed.

I was dropped onto the stretcher and rushed to the ambulance. It took all three Costa Ricans and James to carry me to the ambulance. This was accomplished with much swearing in Spanish, at which James was the most proficient.

Getting my bulk into the cargo bed of the ambulance was trickier for them. Because of my excess weight, the stretcher didn't slide very well. The only way for my small-statured saviors to stuff me in was for one of the attendants to climb inside and straddle the stretcher, facing the open back doors. This position put his crotch less than an inch from my face. The strain of lifting my torso while pulling it further in to the ambulance was a little too much for him, and he farted.

If there was a merciful God, I would have passed out. A fart in close quarters is an unpleasant occurrence by any rational standard of measurement. However, a Costa Rican fart, in a country where the national dish is rice and beans, at one inch, is downright life-threatening. Now it was my turn to swear.

"What's wrong?" yelled James from outside.

"This guy farted," I shot back, eyes watering from the acrid fumes.

"Which one?" he asked. "They all fart." Some days James didn't like where he was. Today was one.

"The one with his hand over his face. Kill the son of a bitch."

"I can't. He's the driver."

"Shit!"

When the back door was closed it almost knocked James flat. He was just climbing into the back to provide support on the way to the clinic in town, our town being too small to deserve a hospital. Closing the door did have at least one positive side to it: Given that I was about three inches longer than the flatbed, I was now very securely wedged into the interior and didn't have to worry about falling off the stretcher. The downside was that, when the door closed, it slammed my head against the partition separating the driver cab from the cargo bed. I passed out again. But I felt lucky; I could no longer smell or feel anything, and I smiled peacefully as James's words grew dimmer in my head.

"Driver or no driver," he was saying, "I should have shot the son of a bitch. We'll both be dead by the time we get to town." I think that for the first time he was enjoying the subtle essence of the driver's fart.

My house is on the side of a mountain in the Tarrazu coffee growing region of Costa Rica and is very remote. The country is mountainous, green with coffee farms, tranquil, blessed with a moderate climate, and populated by generally gentle and loving people. A perfect place to retire. The roads in this region fall into the opposite end of the comfort scale. The road to my house is dirt, full of deep ruts from water runoff and large rocks. Most of which, according to James telling the story later, the driver managed to hit at a good clip on his way into town.

I don't recall much about the ride other than James's comforting voice telling me not to worry, that he was there and everything was going to be fine. His litany kept me attentive rather than giving up the ghost, so to speak. His words, though, were punctuated by two strange sounds every time we hit another boulder. The first was a dull *bong*, followed immediately by a *whop-cush*, and both of them were accompanied by commentary from James regarding the pain he was going to inflict upon the driver if we ever got out of the metal coffin we were in.

"You pig fucker, where did you take driver's training?" was one quote I heard while conscious, over the noise of a very old diesel engine close to death and running at maximum rpm. It was only when we got to the clinic in town and the double back doors were opened allowing light to enter that I figured out what had been going on.

James was sitting on a tool box which rested on the floor. The tool box was about eight inches high and two feet long. Because of his big belly and the lack of headroom he sat with his legs apart crouching forward, cradling his testicles with both hands. He looked a little nauseated. Every time we hit a rock James would be thrown upward slamming his head into the metal ceiling of the ambulance. This was the dull *bong* I kept hearing. His hands couldn't protect his head because they were busy protecting his testicles. The *whop* was his ass and testicles slamming into the tool box upon his descent, and the *crush* was the sound of the tools inside rearranging themselves upon the impact.

The local clinic had a ramp leading down to a loading dock dimly lit by a low wattage single bulb. Dreary during the day and ominous during the night. It had taken all the daylight hours to get the message across that the lone gringo on the mountain could possibly be dead.

When the door opened I saw—through the space between my upturned feet—José, my taxi driver, along with his wife and daughter. They all looked very concerned. I felt embarrassed as I had continued to soil my pants and they could see my soiled condition. I was quickly hauled out and placed upon another gurney. A very unstable James crawled out beside me and, as I was wheeled into the clinic, I could hear him in a loud discussion with the driver. As far as I could tell with my limited Spanish, they were discussing the driver's parentage, educational level, eyesight and lack of hand eye coordination.

I remember the clinic as white and bright. A face appeared over me, listening to my rudimentary Spanish.

"*Yo no mas fuerte*," I kept repeating. I no more strong.

"Speak English," the face responded. Either the face couldn't understand my slurred Spanish or couldn't stand to hear me continue to butcher a beautiful language.

James showed up, his conversation furthering

inter-American relations with the ambulance driver apparently completed, and took over explaining what had happened. I ended up being wheeled into the doctor's office where I kept up my pattern of brief moments of understanding what was going on and longer moments of peacefully passing out.

In retrospect, I now realize that being placed in the doctor's office was the local version of intensive care. If the patient so much as moaned all the doctor had to do was swivel in his chair to be at the bedside. A very effective process.

In one of my lucid moments I remember watching the doctor have an animated conversation on the phone. As the word *gringo* was used a lot, I assumed he was talking about me.

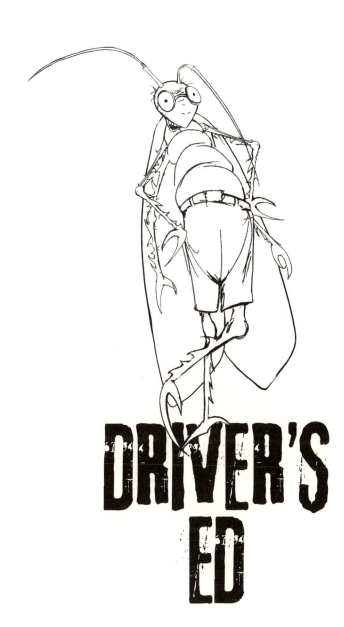

As far as I know, in Costa Rican high schools there are no driver's education courses. As a result, male Costa Ricans appear to drive as they play *futbol*. A rapid dance of cars controlled by salsa music carrying along a driver serene in the knowledge that God and the catholic angels or the plastic Madonna stuck to his dashboard were protecting him. In the United States, if we met with one of them we would be sure the driver was either drunk or trying to commit suicide by inducing those around him into road rage so he could be shot.

On my first visit to Costa Rica we arrived during the evening rush hour. On the way into town I realized that the cars had turned the road's official two lanes into three; with motor cycles whipping between the three imaginary lanes narrowly missing the members of the Salvation Army who were also occupying the conceptual divisions between the impromptu lanes to collect money from the moving cars. All of this was done without the use of horns, swearwords, or gestures. A dangerously graceful highway dance which everyone seemed to understand, while ignoring the possible consequences.

Even with my new understanding and appreciation of God and of the Costa Rican drivers' prowess, I was not prepared for what was to come. Again, I was the lucky one. As I already had one foot in the grave, death would be only a small nudge over the edge. James, though, was as cognizant as he ever was. Which is why he had a deep religious or life-altering experience on our trip in a real Costa Rican ambulance to the hospital in Cartago.

By a "real" ambulance I do not mean on of those monsters that we see in the States. I mean a small Toyota type van that has been converted to an ambulance with some coherent thought behind the conversion process. This one was actually big enough for me. My head and feet still made contact with both ends, but not enough to keep me from rolling off the stretcher when whipping around turns. So, using thin string, my Costa Rican attendants tied me onto the stretcher. There was even a jump seat for James. No more *whop-cush* for him. But still plenty of swearing, this time interspersed with very sincere and reverent praying. Like when you are so hung over you have to get better to die. You know: *God, let me live through this and I'll never drink again.*

The driver of this ambulance was a professional. By which I mean only that his actual job was to drive the *Cruz Roja*, or Red Cross ambulance. Most of the time this was to and from the metropolitan area of the country's capital, San José, where the infirm of our small town could receive greater medical attention than was possible in our remote setting. Other times the trip was one where the vehicle that started the journey as an ambulance ended it as a hearse. I'd screwed up dying, so no hearse was necessary.

This was going to be a trip out of our little valley and up a few thousand feet to the Pan American highway at Empalme. So off we went, James and me in the *Cruz Roja*, José following in his taxi. This wasn't the part that gave James his "come to Jesus" moments, although it did make one realize that it would surely be nice if there was an afterlife.

Just below the Pan American highway where it bisects Empalme, the driver stopped the ambulance, got out, and went into a bar. A stylish establishment with a bare light bulb attached to a downward swan neck metal tube to light the entrance. When I asked James why we were stopping, he replied "The driver needs another beer."

I didn't think this was unusual, so I asked if he would get one for me. James told me it wasn't needed as I was already drunk.

It was the trip *down* the Pan American highway from Empalme into the Cartago area where James's spiritual conversion and life review took place. I was semi-oblivious to the whole thing, so my conversion could wait.

For most of its length, the Pan American highway suffers from a terminal case of potholes. It was cut out of the rain forests some time during the fifties. The result of this half-century old engineering feat was that most of the time one side of the road seemed to simply hang out in mid air. If you went over the edge it would take at least fifteen minutes before you met solid ground. It is the main road north and south in Central America. It wanders from Panama in the South up through Costa Rica, Nicaragua and on up through Mexico. It is always busy with traffic ranging from semi trucks, some new, to bicycles and kamikaze buses. With an occasional cow thrown in for comic relief.

The cows would be tied to a bush or tree alongside the highway to graze on the lush foliage alongside the road. They would occasionally break loose to wander down the road window shopping to select the next spot for dinner. Meeting one of these bovine browsers while traveling well over any reasonable speed limit required a talent for diversion that only a Costa Rican, trained from birth, seems to have.

All of this highway dancing is trickier at night and, on the night of our trip, we had the added benefit of rain and fog, courtesy of the rain forest through which the road had been cut.

On the first severe curve, one of many, the string holding me onto the stretcher broke, depositing me in James's lap. Now James is not normally a physical person, his only exercise being to lift a glass full of gin martinis or, when in Costa Rica, rum. Because of his fastidious approach to his dress, though—something he thought would make people adore him—he was frantic about not getting any of my shit, now oozing out of my trousers, on him. So, in a heroic move, he rolled me back onto the stretcher, holding me in place with his raised foot.

I had always wondered what people meant when describing the passage of time as a blur. Now I know. That was my reality of the drive to the hospital. James's reality was much more credible and life threatening than mine. Although I had begun to realize that I could die. Either from what ever was going on in my body or the ambulance ride. It was just that dying wasn't a big deal any more. I was still in no pain and, as long as there was no pain associated with dying, I reasoned, then dying was no longer of any significance. Which "I" thought this, I don't know.

All I remember of this little sojourn are brief views out the windows by my head of the vegetation whipping by, lit up for a brief moment by the flashing yellow light on top of the ambulance. Like a berserk Con-Ed truck whipping down a country road at ninety miles an hour. It reminded me of being stoned to the bejesus in a dark room where a strobe light would freeze the surroundings for a brief second.

As far as I know the siren was only used once, and could hardly be heard over the steady blare of the engine turning as fast as the driver could push it. In retrospect, it was the perfect way to take this possible trip to the dark side. I had no opinion regarding the proximity of death and was completely at peace with the prospect. James on the other hand emerged from the ride incoherent in both English and Spanish.

At one point during the ride, I recall James surveying the compressed oxygen bottles beside him.

"Fuck it!" he said, to a conspicuously placed placard warning against smoking. "We're all going to die, so I might as well blow us the fuck up and get it over with."

He lit a cigarette. I tried to warn him about the dangers of smoking, but the words became lost in the confusion of the moment. Besides he seemed to enjoy the peace that his available drug of choice gave him.

To James's credit he kept up a steady dialog, like a demented tour guide, telling me where we were at any given moment. His choice of words would quickly have gotten him fired from a stevedore's job. I found myself wanting to hear his voice, as it was something I knew. Otherwise I'd have been content to let the peace of dying overtake me.

When we reached the outskirts of Cartago, the old capital, James's spiel became even more colorful - due in part, I think, to the relief of making it down the mountains in one piece while still breathing.

Occasionally, he'd insist I peer out my window quickly.

"One of the world's top three trophy asses coming up on your side," was the usual reason.

I didn't know how he was rating this or that particular female bottom without knowing who the first runner up might be, let alone the winner, but on his command I would look out the side window to see the senorita he admired.

The ambulance finally stopped.

"We made it," James said. "You're okay now, buddy. We're at the hospital in Cartago." He was speaking more in relief than to keep me informed.

Viewed through the space between my feet as the back doors were opened, it was just another loading dock lit by a dim bulb designed for the infirm or dying. I was rushed inside where more faces appeared, accompanied by painful prodding and poking. Somewhere during the trip my body must have decided to override my brain and let me know there was pain associated with what ever the hell was wrong with me. Later my entire left side would become so sensitive that even clothing touching my skin there would cause great pain.

After what seemed only a few minutes I was put back into the ambulance, James again at my side.

"What happened?" I said. "Where are we going?"

"You smell too bad. They're sending you to another hospital for a bath and a CAT scan."

To my muddled brain this registered as "bat can" and, all the way to the second hospital in San Jose I tried to figure out just what I was in for. I didn't get it until I was pushed into the bat can machine and told to lie still. As if I had a choice. I still hadn't figured how to get anything to move. Evidently I was still having little strokes to further debilitate me. Just like earthquake aftershocks. Until these stopped, I was still in danger of leaving this world after too brief a stay.

Out of the machine, people entering and leaving my field of view, counting ceiling tiles to keep myself comfortable, I had joined Alice in her Wonderland.

Faces reappeared, speaking Spanish. James translating, "Follow the finger." This turned out to be more difficult than you'd think.

Pins stuck in my right arm. "Ouch."

Pins stuck in my left arm. "What are you doing?"

Back into the ambulance. Back to my never ending journey.

I don't remember the ride back to the first hospital in Cartago, possibly due to the drugs I'd been given, but I remember my second arrival there with a covey of white dressed people pushing me around, a needle stuck in the back of my useless left hand.

At one point James reappeared, out of breath and sweating.

"How am I doing?" I asked.

"You're a cabbage that's shat in its pants," James replied in his best bedside manner. "You've had a stroke.

In fact, you've had three of them. You're lucky to be breathing. I think I can get the government to cover the hospital bill."

With that I went to sleep for a day or two, actually a week. I found out years later why James was out of breath and sweating.

While at the second hospital for my bat can James talked José into taking him to the closest bar for several shots of rum and a few *bocas*, small bites of food served with drinks.

James was severely stressed. The only other person in the valley that spoke English and could match him shot for shot was dying or already dead. In his mind this was a life altering event.

After enough rum to steady his nerves, James was ready to get back in the game. He and José returned to the bat can hospital. When James asked the person in admitting where they had put the *gringo*, he was told that they did not have any *gringos* staying with them.

James does not handle rejection well and started his ugly American act. He demanded that they search the entire hospital for his valuable friend.

In the meantime José, who had had just a few shots of rum to be social, wandered out to the dock where the ambulances delivered their cargo.

After talking to the drivers, he learned that one of their compadres had taken the body back to Cartago.

IN THE BEGINNING THERE WERE MARTINIS

The defining moment leading to my attempt to retire in Costa Rica occurred during a very drunk New Year's celebration some five or six years before my slow down call from God.

I'd become friends with James several years earlier. He was a senior technical representative for a very large computer manufacturer. I was working for a bank that used many of his company's products. We both lived on Bainbridge Island in Washington's Puget Sound and worked in Seattle and, though we didn't know each other formally, we would both often be on the same ferry boat to or from work so knew each other by sight.

One night James was out for dinner and drinks with a guy from his company, the representative who handled my employer's account. During dinner the bank rep mentioned that I lived on Bainbridge also. James indicated that he knew where I lived and that they all should drop by and say hello. I don't think the other rep really understood what he was agreeing to as James piled everyone on his boat for more drinks during the trip to my house.

My house was right on the water of Puget Sound, my back yard ending at the waters edge with a fantastic view of Seattle. My wife and I had just gone to bed and were almost asleep when someone started sounding a boat horn. One of those aerosol can boat horns that can be heard over the roar of a jet engine. After several minutes it became obvious that whoever had the damn thing would not stop until told to do so. Being the head of the house it was my job to wander down stairs and express my displeasure as well as that of my neighbors.

When I turned on the flood lights to the back yard, I was greeted by a rather large, very white ass bobbing not twenty feet off shore. I was being mooned.

Riley, meet James. I now knew the ass and the following morning on the ferry it introduced the face that went with it.

The relationship that developed between us was bizarre at best. Whenever we would get together we would get into trouble. Either with our spouses, individuals closest to us during our performance art show, or with the institution we were visiting.

One time James's wife invited me to a birthday party for James. I haven't sung happy birthday to James since then. The highlight of the evening was the presentation of a very large chocolate mousse cake his wife had commissioned especially for the occasion. Unfortunately by the time it was presented to the assembled guests James and I were well in the bag.

The cake was placed on a stool in the middle of the kitchen while we all sang Happy Birthday. As the music died James surveyed the elaborately decorated morsel with somewhat bleary eyes. He cut the cake with a karate chop right in the middle, sending a large portion onto the floor. I and his teenage daughter, a magnificent full bodied girl, reacted quickly, grabbing as much of the cake off the floor as we could. She, possessed of her fathers genes, quickly decided that I would look better wearing the cake all over my face. I had the exact same impulse, and we proceeded to smear each other with the goo. Not wanting to be bested by a mere teenager, I grabbed another handful, held her firmly with my other hand, and inserted the gloop down the inside of her sweater, smearing it back and forth between her two large breasts like a windshield wiper and really enjoying the feel of her slippery breasts or as much of them as the constraints of her bra would allow. All of this was photographed by her mother, recording the occasion for the family photo album.

James, on the other hand, was not so violent. One night, at a formal dinner party in honor of a member of the Swedish diplomatic corps, James found himself seated in the middle of the long dinner table. His chair was only a few inches away from a piece of furniture which prevented him from getting out of his chair while people sat next to him.

Having an urgent need to relieve himself of the many cocktails he'd enjoyed before dinner, he pushed his chair back as far as he could and slid quietly under the table, where he roamed about for some time.

As I was topside with an unobstructed view of all the guests, most of whom were female, I could chart James's progress by the startled expressions on the women's faces, some of them expressing obvious pleasure. In a short time he emerged on the opposite side of the table from where he started, stood up, dusted his knees off and announced loudly, "I know which ladies are wearing panties and which ones aren't."

James and I left early.

The New Year's Eve get-together that would be a defining moment in my life was going as well as could be expected. I was the only one on time. Every one but me worked in town. I was working out of my house. I would watch a ferry boat come in to our harbor from Seattle, and figured that I could enjoy a martini while the rest of the celebration disembarked and came to pick me up. After watching four ferry arrivals and departures I had started the New Year before any one else. I was bombed. Once we got to the restaurant, though, everyone else caught up with me in no time. The maitre de even offered us a free taxi ride home before we had eaten.

Sometime toward the end of the evening when we were all completely incoherent, James informed us that he and his wife were building a retirement home in Costa Rica. For some reason important only to him he stated that I should go down there with him on his next trip to check it out. I was the only one that didn't think too highly of the idea. My protestations were met with all sorts of drunken counter arguments that seemed to make sense at the time. Finally, in an attempt to quiet everyone down, I agreed. I thought that everyone would forget about the whole thing once we recovered in the light of the New Year.

Around January fourth or fifth, James appeared at my front door and handed me an envelope.

"What's this?" I asked.

"It's a non-refundable, round trip ticket to Costa Rica," he said. "You owe me seven hundred forty-three dollars and change."

Oh God, what have I done? I thought in panic as he turned and headed for his truck parked in the driveway.

"When are we going?" I shouted.

"March."

I didn't even open the envelope. A lot could happen before March. I could have a second appendectomy. I put the envelope in that kitchen drawer we all have, the one full of rubber bands, matchbooks, one shoelace, nuts and bolts, the emergency flashlight with long-dead batteries, expired coupons cut from the Sunday paper. That's where the ticket belonged, I figured. Perhaps it would get lost.

I forgot about the whole thing until one day in late February. I was returning home from seeing a client, and caught James sneaking home on an early ferry.

"You excited?" he asked, sitting down at my booth in the galley with two beers and pushing one in my direction.

"About what?" I said, completely perplexed.

"Costa Rica, you asshole."

"Oh, shit," I said. "I completely forgot. Can't go. Too much work." Stretching the truth just a tad.

"You have no choice, you're out seven hundred bucks," James said. "I've made all the reservations, and to cancel will cost me a fortune. And, besides, your wife is planning on having an affair in your absence."

"Well, in that case," I said, "I guess I'm going." There was something in his voice that told me he was serious about losing the money. I'd find out later he was also right about the affair.

I spent the next couple of weeks making excuses to clients, buying film and clothes suitable for the tropics, getting passport photos taken, and generally running around like a chicken with its head cut off.

The day before I was scheduled to leave, I thought it prudent to look at my ticket so I would know how much of my blood pressure medicine to take with me. It was only then I discovered that my flight left at 12:15 AM, a redeye flight through Dallas to Miami (where I was meeting James, who'd left days earlier on business). I also discovered we'd be out of the country for almost a month. The son-of-a-bitch had sandbagged me again. I began planning his immediate and painful death.

I do not fit in a normal seat on an airplane. Most of my six foot five height is between my rear end and my knees. I literally become lodged in the seat, my knees protruding a good three inches into the back of the person sitting in front of me; that is, if the seats are soft backed. On planes equipped with stiff backed seats, my butt doesn't hit bottom. A painful way to spend a night.

Even with an emergency exit row seat, which I'd successfully pestered the departure gate agent into putting me in, I still got no sleep on the flight to Miami.

Arriving at mid morning I quickly went into culture shock. Miami was hot and muggy and no-one was speaking English. It was all Spanish, and well beyond the half dozen or so words I knew. To make it even more perfect, I was wearing my Seattle summer outfit, summer in Seattle topping out at around fifty degrees. No sleep. Hot and sweaty. James was definitely going to pay.

Our flight from Miami to San Jose Costa Rica was on their national carrier LACSA. I found the ticket counter, checked my bags, and found a place to sit across from the gate on the floor against a wall. The floor and the wall were much cooler than my body temperature, and felt great. A fine location from which to ambush James.

It took three hours for him to show up, dragging behind him one of those collapsible carts with roller blade wheels that are advertised to glide smoothly down the aisle of an airplane but in real life end up being carried sideways to the assigned seat. He was wearing a sweater stretched tight over his ample beer belly. He was smiling. I was not.

"Isn't this great?" he said, waving his arms to indicate the surroundings.

"You son-of-a-bitch," I said.

"I see you're enjoying the trip so far," he said, cutting me off before I could get him in my sights for a full broadside. "Let me check my bags, then we can chat."

He disappeared into the swirling crowd to emerge later after I had cooled down a bit. His timing was always good when I was ready to tear into him.

We went in search of a spot to buy a beer. When we found one it was some distance from our starting point. As we settled into our seats I finally had my chance to express my sincere and heartfelt feelings.

"You're buying, you slut," I said. "My flight left at midnight and I haven't slept a wink."

"Quit your griping," he said. "This is exciting. We're on our way to Costa Rica, old buddy!"

James's excitement was genuine. And infectious. I was soon caught up in the moment, getting drunk on the beers that kept arriving and having one hell of a lot of fun. James and I were like a free-association comedy act, each feeding off the other until we were constantly laughing.

Our flight and gate number were announced. I spotted a gate number not far from us and we finished off the last round of beers and hurried to the gate. We were met by two very attractive Latin women, to whom we offered our tickets and hurried down the gang way. We were almost on board when I asked the man in line in front of me, "How long is the flight to San José?"

"San José?" he said. "We're going to San Paulo, Brazil."

Going against the flow of those going to Brazil, we made it back to the two pretty women and James, talking in rapid Spanish, somehow got our tickets back.

Needless to say, we were the last to board the flight to San José, where we each had bulkhead aisle seats across from each other, with another passenger inside us at the window seat. James, seasoned international traveler, knew that on this part of the trip the drinks were free and quickly ordered us a round to tamp down the beers we had just finished.

Shortly after takeoff we each received four little bottles of booze. Now we could fly with the aircraft if we worked it right. My seatmate turned out to be a very nice gentleman who was the comptroller of the airline and we were soon in conversation about the wonders of Costa Rica and the country's largest export crop, coffee. One of my clients at the time was a very large coffee company headquartered in Seattle so I was trying to sell the gentleman on exclusively using my client's Costa Rican roast on his airline.

James's seatmate was also a business man. Their conversation was much louder than ours, mostly in Spanish. After one particularly loud outburst from the two of them I turned to see what all the commotion was about. James winked and made a circle with his index finger and thumb. On exiting the plane we let our seatmates go first. I told James about my seatmate and what I had been negotiating with him. James had been negotiating too. His seatmate ran a whorehouse. I did not know that prostitution was a legal enterprise in Costa Rica.

I was like a little kid on the way to our hotel. The sun was shining, a gentle breeze blowing, and the temperature comfortably warm. I was filled with excitement at the possibilities of this new adventure and starting to think that maybe this trip might be alright after all.

Our hotel was what we call in the States a boutique hotel. Off the beaten path but quaint, it was the converted mansion of one of the country's long gone presidents. James and I were given the bridal suite, though I had trouble believing this as it had two single beds.

The room was large by any standards, complete with cable TV. The ceiling was of wood that resembled black walnut. Very striking in appearance. The bathroom and its anteroom both boasted wallpaper that had big splashes of aqua blue and two foot long raindrops of shiny silver. The silver portions acted like mirrors that reflected whatever portion of the body they were nearest to. The paper covered all the walls, the ceiling, and even the toilet tank so that it blended into the wall. Drunk or sober, you thought you were hallucinating every time you went to the John.

After we unpacked, James took me on a private tour to introduce me to all the people he knew at the hotel, including the ex-pat American owner, the bartender who knew what James wanted to drink without being told, and the desk clerk who mentioned that Maria would be thrilled to know James was back in town, she only recently having been released from jail. It was a grand tour.

The gift shop, which spilled out of itself into the

hallways and seating areas, had a large collection of wood carvings that resembled chainsaw art and one particular carving caught our eye. It was a life size bust of Jesus, a crown of thorns puncturing his forehead, blood trickling down his face, and his eyes turned heavenward with a pleading look. James thought it would look good in the lobby of my bank. We got the giggles thinking up ways that we could have it presented to the bank in a manner that would force them to display it in the lobby of their corporate headquarters. We might have had too much to drink.

After several more rounds at the bar, James informed me that it was time to get cured. Of what, I had no idea, but off we went, James leading at a good clip, his flailing arms constantly in motion as he described what he felt were points of interest. I followed him down streets that made me very uncomfortable, populated with swarthy characters who looked as if, given the opportunity, they'd slit your throat to take your shoes. James was oblivious to all of this, forcing congregations of these people to part so we could pass, all of them viewing our passage with surly looks that frightened the hell out of me.

"Take a look at this," James said, standing in front of a multi-storied building and gesturing at it. We'd passed through the dimly lit unsavory part of town and were now amongst normal looking people. "Isn't it great?"

"What's great about it?" I said, unimpressed. "It looks like a building to me."

"It's metal," he said, hitting the side of the building

with a rock he'd picked up. It clanged in response. "It's a school, still in use today. It was cast in France and shipped around the Horn on sailing ships sometime in the late eighteen hundreds. It's bolted together. Isn't it great?"

I had to admit it kind of was.

After several more minutes of wandering, we made it to one of the main streets of the capital, four to six lanes wide, with stores and cafés on one side and a park and cathedral on the other.

"This is it," James proclaimed and darted into a café fronting this main street. I followed obediently and we took a seat at a table where we could watch the people passing. It was early evening by now and it seemed as if those out walking were doing so as a custom, in no hurry, out to enjoy the evening. A waitress appeared and James ordered us both *Sopa Negro con hombre completo.*

"What did you just order?" I asked, as she left.

"Black bean soup with a whole man."

"What the hell does that mean?"

"Two eggs," he said. "Half a man gets you only one egg."

This exchange took some time to sink in. Maybe I'd drunk too much.

"This'll cure you," James said, when the soup arrived. "Drink this and you won't have a hangover in the morning."

The soup was delicious, with the "whole man", two hard boiled eggs, floating just under the surface. We enjoyed our meal in silence, our exertions of a very long day catching up with us. We sat for several hours, enjoying the excellent coffee that followed the meal.

I noticed that there seemed to be three distinct stages to the men I saw out walking in the cooling night. First, the teenagers, loud, swaggering, wearing gang type clothing, and single. Second, the young men with beautiful Costa Rican girls on their arms. The last were the men with a woman on one arm and a baby in the other. They were proud, nodding to their friends, stopping to talk in subdued tones with others. Admiring the children no matter what the age. Things are the same the world over, I thought.

After dinner we made it back to the hotel through the same threatening streets. A quick stop at the bar for a night cap, then off to bed. A peaceful first evening in a foreign land coming to an end.

SLEEPING WITH JESUS

The next morning I awoke to the word of the Lord.

"You must accept Jesus into your life or you will burn in eternal damnation," said a mournful, almost spectral voice, penetrating my jet-lag dreams.

I floated up toward consciousness, my eyes still closed.

"You have sinned against God," the voice said. "Repent or you will burn in hell."

The voice sounded awfully close.

"You have sinned. You have recommended the purchase of non-IBM equipment."

Wait a minute. I opened my eyes. And found myself face to face with Jesus. He was lying in the bed next to mine.

I jerked upright...and finally realized what was going on.

The bastard formerly known as James, not needing as much catch-up sleep as me, had been up with the birds to sneak through the deserted corridors to the gift shop and swipe the bust of Jesus. He'd put it on his pillow, fluffing up his covers so it looked like Jesus was sleeping in his bed, and then lay down on the floor on the far side of his bed to start his ghostly sermon. Nice.

We spent the next few days walking around the capital. James knew all the places tourists should not go. We paid a visit to them all. He also knew of many places a tourist would be lucky to visit. We had superb food in small cafés I wouldn't go into at first. Garlic soup that wasn't on the menu. Roast pork to die for in a sidewalk cafe populated by swarthy men who were illegal money changers, each carrying hundreds of thousands of U. S. dollars in briefcases, some with large friends in attendance to ensure the money stayed where it should.

After three day of touring, James told me to pack my bags as we were off to the interior to evaluate the progress of his house. We went to catch a *directo,* a bus that supposedly went directly to our destination without stopping.

The bus station was a thing of beauty. A tin building painted sky blue in a very rundown part of town. The bus, a retired school bus from the States, bore the name *Donna Maria* in large orange letters which really stood out against the lime green of the rest of the bus.

A small electric fan on the dash pointed at the driver's seat. A statue of the Virgin Mary next to the fan pointed at the passengers. The seat spacing made a commuter airplane look downright roomy. James and I settled into the last seat across the back of the bus, with our feet in the central aisle. The only place either of us fit. Before long the bus was full. Full of passengers, but missing a driver. As we all sat there, the interior getting uncomfortably warm from the midmorning sun and the bodies packed into the thing, James and I spent the time admiring the young women trying to outdo each other with their suggestive dress. A paradise for dirty old men.

After an hour or so, the driver was finally located and persuaded to get on board. Finally we were on our way, whipping at great speed down narrow streets, through residential areas not used to bus traffic, and on to the outskirts where we joined the midday traffic climbing the mountains that surround San José.

Traveling the fabled Pan American Highway, I was enthralled. I had never seen such a beautiful place. It reminded me of where I was stationed in Africa while in the service. The mountains went straight up and still had blue green coffee bushes planted on the vertical sides. In this brief moment I had fallen in love with the country.

On first sight, I wasn't too impressed with what was soon to be my new home town. Good sized with a two block business section, the center of much commerce, most of it dealing with the growing and processing of coffee.

Our hotel had a restaurant occupying its ground floor. It was supposed to be Chinese, but I'm not sure a Chinese person would recognize black beans and rice with soy sauce as something his or her mother would make.

My room was elegant by Costa Rican country standards, only one bed and a double bed at that, but the bathroom was a different story altogether. The sink had no trap, the bend in the pipe beneath the sink required by USA building codes. The trap's purpose is to let water collect in the bend and seal off the pipe to escaping sewer gas. The lack of this bend was what gave the rooms their distinctive aroma. A smell I could never get used to.

The shower was unique. The water was heated by passing through an electric coil in a device that looked like a pregnant shower head. Bare wires led to a bare switch on the shower wall that turned it on. There was no way to turn it on without getting in the stall, which meant you were standing naked with your feet in water. I found that three or four beers made the experience less threatening.

During the summer months, the town could run out of water by midmorning. The owners of the hotel had installed two large fiberglass tanks on the roof which would fill during the night when water was plentiful.

James and I occupied the last two rooms at the end of an open breezeway. The pipes and valves from the roof tanks were just out of sight on the outside of the building and could be opened or closed by reaching through an iron lattice at the end of the breezeway. When you ran out of water mid-shower, you had to get out, run to the lattice, reach out, and open the valve to the second tank of water before the shower head turned into a hot mass of bubbling plastic.

This little drill was always dangerous as the floors were tiled and well polished. But at least it let you display your nude body to the other guests if they were arriving or departing when the water ran out.

JAMES GREETS THE GUESTS

One morning I went to the pharmacy across the street to get some tooth paste and, returning, was confronted by an obviously distressed hotel manager. I understood nothing of his rapid-fire Spanish and turned to the gathering crowd of shoppers.

"Does any one here speak English?" I asked.

An attractive middle aged woman agreed to interpret for me, and the manager started over.

"He says that Costa Rica has laws for handling perverts and exhibitionists," said the woman.

"What the fuck is he talking about?" I said.

"Sir," she said, "I will not translate that type of language."

I apologized and asked her to tell him that I didn't understand. She talked to him. He talked to her. She turned back to me.

"Your friend exposed himself to children this morning," she said. "The parents are filing a complaint with the police at this very moment."

The Manager wasn't done talking.

"He says they don't want people like you in the hotel," my interpreter said.

"Wait a minute," I said, not knowing where else I could sleep. "I have no idea what's going on, but if it concerns my friend, then I'm sure it's just a misunderstanding. He's harmless. Nuts, but harmless."

The interpreter and the Manager had another little chat, this time in more subdued tones.

"Is the man mentally ill?" the woman asked.

"Oh yes," I said. "Very. But he's completely harmless. His medication causes him to be a little more erratic than most gringos. He is very proud of his manhood."

My translator had a little difficulty with that one and even more with the Manager's response.

"He says that from what the mother told him, your friend has no reason for his pride." She was blushing a little. "The manager also asks if he has ever assaulted any one?"

"No!" I said, emphatically. "Deep down he's a pacifist and doesn't condone any sort of physical confrontation."

She passed this on and gave me the Manager's answer.

"He says that as long as he is harmless and no one was really hurt, you both can stay. But the fat one must keep his clothes on at all times"

I expressed my sincere and profound thanks to both the manager and my translator and agreed to monitor James's wardrobe.

I finally found out what had happened during cocktail hour that evening. As James and I sat on the hotel's small balcony overlooking the street, drinking a Chilean burgundy and eating anchovies, James showed me a large lump on the back of his head.

That morning, eager to get to his construction site, he'd run out of water after starting his shower. He left his room all lathered up, ran to the lattice, and turned on the valve. Running back to his room he slipped on the tile, fell backwards, and knocked himself out. There he lay sopping wet, face up, arms and legs outstretched, completely exposing himself to any arriving or departing guests.

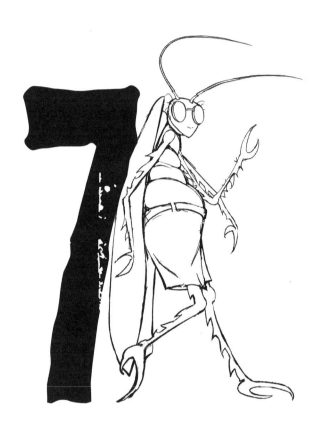

A HOME IN PAIR OF DICE

Every morning, James would leave me and head up to his construction site. At first I would hang around the hotel waiting for him to return so I could go get some breakfast. I soon learned that James used his fluency in Spanish for his benefit only. He could give a shit whether I could order food in a restaurant. I became superfluous to his daily routine during our time in town.

One morning I inadvertently mentioned something to James. "I could live here," I said.

That was all it took. A taxi ride lasting the better part of the day took us on a tour of land for sale. I saw many parcels, some good, some bad. Late in the day, we came to a parcel about four kilometers from town.

Almost ten acres of land on the South face of a mountain, with water available from a spring higher up. It was one of those serendipitous occasions that you react to with your soul and not your mind. There was no hesitation. No doubt. I belonged in this place.

"I'll take it," I said.

My wife and I had already gone through the legal niceties of a separation which I had hoped would induce her to reconsider her actions. So I guess that when I saw the land, she was no longer a consideration in my future plans, even though I did not recognize it at the time. There would be plenty of anger and pain following the divorce.

The owner of the land, an elfin little man who could drink a grizzly under the table, was the father in law of José, the taxi driver. The price and terms were right so, pending the sale of my house on Bainbridge Island, a deal was quickly struck.

The rest of our visit to this magical land was just as spontaneous and offbeat. James swimming with sharks at one of the nation's many parks. James in a remote cantina, leaning against the bar having a serious conversation with a four year old girl whose feet didn't reach the topmost rung on the bar stool she occupied. Bus and taxi rides to turn your hair white. Medicines to cure your sniffles that would leave you hallucinating for hours. James was a gifted and inspired tour guide. I was lucky to get out of the country alive. As the years have passed and I have learned more about James's tour through this life I am amazed that he is still upright and taking nourishment, legal or illegal. Someone should have shot him years ago.

24 HOUR NURSING CARE AND SALSA MUSIC

"Banana sí, banana no, banana come, banana go."

What the hell was going on? First, there was nothing. I mean, I was there but there were no senses, no light, no smells or sounds, no feeling. Just peace, love, warmth and blackness. Then all this peaceful nothingness was shattered by the sounds of young female voices singing joyfully about bananas. I preferred the nothingness, more peaceful, less effort. The young female voices kept up their joyous singing. "Banana large, banana small, banana short, banana tall."

Somewhere, it dimly registered that they really weren't singing about bananas.

Then, to a Latin beat, another song started somewhere off to my right, not as loud but just as happy. Sensory overload alert. It was getting too confusing, even though I sensed that these songs were coming from radios.

"Senor, usted seco?" This was not a song but a real voice in my ear.

Feeling began. Still no light but, slowly, I became aware of pain as I started to regain consciousness. The more awake I got, the stronger the pain. I was nudged on my right shoulder, and felt the pain strongly on my entire left side. *Oh hell*, I thought, *I give up*. And I opened my eyes.

I was in a bed in a large room, a hospital ward with sixteen beds. I was flanked on each side by a beautiful *Tica*, the slang name for a Costa Rican woman. Both were dressed in white uniforms. With my first view on opening my eyes being lots of whiteness and two beautiful women, I briefly felt I might be where we all hope to end up.

I tried to move my body further up in the bed. My feet were against the bedstead at the foot of the bed causing great pain in my left foot. The two young women helped by sliding their arms under my torso and lifting. When there was no longer any contact the pain lessened but did not go away.

This was my first experience of having my body moved about by women. After two hospitals and many months of confinement I have learned that women handle a body differently than men. They lift the body, while men grab it and pull. Women do it better.

"Usted seco?" one of the nurses asked again. I could only look at her. The need to reply hadn't registered yet.

"Usted pee pee?" she said. That one I got.

"Yes. Ugh, sí," I said, realizing that I had indeed pee peed when I felt the dampness in my crotch.

Before I could protest, I was nude. These two little angels had obviously undressed a man in bed before. I was much more concerned with my naked state than they were. Costa Rican women have been taking care of their males from childhood on, so a naked guy was nothing to them. No need for a modesty towel over the genitals. Just let it all hang out.

They quickly set about giving me a bath, using so much water that I couldn't call it a sponge bath. The mattresses were waterproof and all the sheets and towels soaked up the water. I was handed a soapy wash cloth and instructed to clean my own banana. I did so to the refrain of "Banana fat, banana thin, I love the shape my banana's in."

While washing my banana I noticed several women

looking through the windows lining the corridor a few feet from my bed. A cleaning Lady mopping the floor at the foot of my bed had stopped to watch, too. I was on display. I guess the *Ticas* wanted to see if Gringos really had barbed dicks or something. My banana washing went as quickly as possible notwithstanding the pain caused by every movement of my good arm and hand.

When I finished with my banana, the nurse on the right poured water on it for rinsing. She did so from a good height above me. Like a show-off waiter pouring a glass of water by holding the pitcher above his head and the glass at his waist. It really felt strange having your banana react to the falling water. She could make it twirl, first in one direction, then the other. Like a stripper rotating her tassels. I wondered how much practice it took before she could master this little trick. I was somewhat taken aback when this occurred but could think of nothing to say or do so I kept quiet and attempted to act cool, as though having my banana twirled was an every day occurrence.

There should be instructions for young boys of reading age on the proper etiquette for banana twirling. Or for being the recipient of a banana twirl. It's something that every person in possession of a banana should know in order to avoid any social *faux pas*.

My large female audience seemed to enjoy the banana twirling portion of my cleansing the most. I know that most of the dirty old men in this world would think it a blessing to be bathed by two such beautiful creatures. I'd think so too, but unfortunately there was too much pain involved. My entire left side was super sensitive, especially to touch, and by the time I'd been cleaned to their high standards my eyes were watering from the pain.

Once my *tica* angels were satisfied, I was clothed like the other inmates in hospital type pajama bottoms held up with a drawstring, in my case not quite meeting in the middle or reaching to my ankles. The man next to me was wearing my pajamas; more than large enough to encircle him twice, his hands and feet completely out of sight in the sleeves and legs. It would be a week before any one would correct the dressing problem.

My bed was first to the right when you entered the room, a few feet from the windows lining the corridor, so I was given the first pair of pajamas in the pile given to the washwomen. The large pair was the second pair down so it naturally belonged to the second person to be bathed every morning.

The poor guy would somehow manage to get the foot or so of extra sleeve caught under his body so he couldn't move until he got the attention of one of the nurses. They'd cheerfully pull his arm out from under him and continue their work, but within a few moments he would again be bound up as if wearing a straitjacket and begin to call for help in a very weak voice. This became one of the many daily dramas to occupy each day.

After the entire ward was bathed, we were fed. As I soon discovered, we had our own kitchen and cooks. The hospital was designed with each ward having its own kitchen and cooks with it. The cooks both cooked the food and then served it. There wasn't too much griping about the food as the cooks, very stout women with matching demeanors, quickly silenced any complaints like mothers scolding little children for being fussy eaters. Very effective. It's hard to complain directly to the face that had just labored to fix your meal, especially if you're conditioned from birth to believe that the provider of food is a good person not to be offended by your feeble complaints.

I now started my individual training course on how to get a body that only responded to commands on one side to do what you want it to do. Scooting up in the bed by grabbing the headboard with my right hand and simultaneously pulling with my right arm while pushing with my right foot was no small feat. The damage to my brain made any physical effort exhausting. It seemed to rob my good side of the strength it once had. Believe me, moving an arm and a leg as dead weight is extremely difficult, particularly when that dead weight feels like it's about a ton.

I soon learned to identify the very small gains that were made daily. One day while trying to roll onto my right shoulder the left part of my torso stayed behind. The next day I would tighten my stomach muscles and it would roll with me. I quickly learned to forget trying to do anything that involved my left side. One of the fortuitous things about my stroke was that its impact was on my non-dominant side. Being right handed made things a little easier during recovery. I don't want to think about the condition I'd have been in if it had been my right side that was affected.

As it was, my left eye drooped. The left side of my face was completely slack, which gave a particular lilt to my spoken Spanish as well as my native tongue. In addition, I was quite adept at drooling. I wouldn't realize it was happening until I felt the coolness on my chin from the saliva making its way downstream. At first I was very embarrassed, but soon got over it when I noticed that I was in a room populated by expert droolers. A good half of the inmates in this room had suffered strokes, while the other half seemed to be recovering alcoholics. The alcoholics were the ones with the dueling radios. They were also the best droolers.

My left shoulder was three to four inches lower than my right as there were no nerves firing off to keep the muscles tense. The left arm, totally useless, was forever staying put when the rest of me moved. My left arm and hand were my own personal Harry. Hit the ball (body), drag Harry (the arm).

Costa Ricans love music and radios, which can apparently only function in one of two states: either completely off, or turned to maximum volume, no matter what the hour of day. I suffered from hospital sleep deprivation for the first week of my confinement. I would learn later that "Hospital sleep deprivation" is a real life technical term. The staff that worked this ward all loved their music and would join in with the singing whenever the mood overtook them, day or night. Despite my sleep issues, it was a great, happy, loving environment.

It was this happy loving environment that seemed to be the big difference between the care I received in Costa Rica and the care I received in the States. In the States the happiness had definite boundaries, the loving care institutionalized. I have never felt cared for by strangers as I did in Costa Rica. This applied not only to the staff but to complete strangers as well. Strangers would take time from visiting their own friends or family to wish me luck.

One time an old man, old enough to give an eyewitness account of the big bang, was visiting an inmate from a neighboring town who was in the bed next to mine. Recognizing me as someone who lived close by, the old man came over to me and softly stroked my forehead. Speaking slowly and softly, he told me that he had prayed for me and that God was taking care of me, that because of his prayers I would be all right. It was a lovely caring gesture that moved me deeply. The effects of this kind of care made me feel protected and safe as if in a cocoon of spirit that could not be breached by the vicissitudes of modern life. I still feel that today. I have since learned that this feeling is not uncommon with people who have been blessed with an out of body experience.

About halfway through my first morning of coherency, Dr. Muños arrived to see me. He was a tall and handsome man, distinguished and with a regal bearing. I liked him immediately. Because of my stroke, I liked everyone immediately. It had been he that had taken charge of me and had pulled me through to this point. He had received his training in Romania and had specialized in strokes, another coincidence in my favor. With his arrival came the greetings. All the nurses would approach him in turn and bid him good morning by kissing him on the cheek, a greeting usually reserved for family members and very close friends, though I didn't know this at the time. Those nurses who went first were actually female doctors; they dressed in the same white as the nurses so it was hard to tell them apart.

The doctor approached my bed. "Como esta?" he said. How are you. He picked up my arm and pulled the stint out of the back of my left hand. He did so at an angle that I thought would tear open a gash in my skin, but the stint was white plastic that bent under my skin's strength.

Trying my best with what little Spanish I knew, I responded, "Yo en cama con Dolores."

I was trying to say that I was in bed with pain, *dolor* being the Spanish word for pain. Instead, I'd told him that I was in bed with a woman named Dolores—which may or may not have been a painful experience.

He responded with glee. "Similar con Lupe," he said. Just like Lupe. With that the female nurse or doctor standing next to him uttered a small squeak, turned scarlet and smacked him on the arm, more in surprise than embarrassment. She seemed quite proud that the good doctor had made this joke. I think there might have been some truth to the statement. Or maybe it was just that by making the joke the good doctor was finally moving to her wavelength. Either way the response was cute and fun.

I tried to explain about the pain on my left side. Also, that my left leg had started to misbehave. It would have a violent spasm wherein the knee would jerk up as the big toe tried to bend back on itself and try to touch my instep, a very painful spasm that, no matter how hard I tried, I could not stop. These spasms still visit me today although not as frequently. They have been so violent as to scrape the skin and meat off my left shin when they occurred while my foot was under a table.

On hearing about my spasms he nodded thoughtfully and spoke rapidly to the now composed Lupe. The good doctor had dismissed me. Or so I thought. With lunch that afternoon, I was given a large quantity of pills which I managed to get down. Swallowing was also not working well. But that is what started this little journey. It took thirty minutes or so for the pills to kick in. Then I really started enjoying my stay.

If you are to believe every thing he wrote, I had just started the Hunter S. Thompson Gonzo Journalist's method of survival: Accept all drugs offered and always ask for more.

The drugs really did help my powers of observation, though. Things seemed to get a little bizarre there for a while. Colors were a bit more vibrant, mosquitoes a bit louder on their inbound approach. Time became a little hard to keep track of in this new hallucinogenic reality. It was now just a fun continuum filled with all sorts of weird happy surprises and with no pain. The nurses seemed even more sensual, if that was possible, and the rest of the day practically flew by.

The next day James resurfaced to tell me he had contacted my ex-wife and my eldest son. They were both trying to get a flight to Costa Rica as soon as possible to be with me. Though this would prove difficult, because the tourist season was winding down and all flights in and out of Costa Rica were booked solid, I finally had something to look forward to other than my daily bath and its growing crowd of onlookers. I took my morning ration of drugs and tried to picture the reunion with the ex while in my drug induced euphoric state. I realized I would need to be quiet or I might do something rash like proposing to her again.

While he was there, James engaged the doctor in a lengthy conversation. James always assumed an aura of profound interest when talking with a Costa Rican of high status. This was either out of respect or the fact he didn't understand a thing they were saying. Their conversation concerned my present condition and prognosis for recovery. It must not have been too good because James became very somber.

His reaction was just something I observed, rather than something I was bothered by. The drugs were starting to take effect. I was concentrating alternately on the flight of incoming mosquitoes and on the semi-nude nurse who only I seemed able to see, as no one else in the room took any notice of her. It occurred to me to beckon her over and ask for seconds on my morning allotment of drugs so that I could view her almost naked beauty up close. But I gave it up for some more sleep.

Sleep was something that seemed to occur quite often. I don't know if it was drug induced or a reaction of my body trying to recover from the assault it had undergone. I would be cruising along just fine in the real world when, wham, I'd hit a wall and was instantly completely exhausted. Time for beddy-bye.

For the most part, I didn't dream during these periods of sleep. I was *there*, somehow, but was enveloped in nothingness, an unthreatening black void that felt like it was supposed to be there, comforting me during my visits to this peaceful place.

Waking up was always a surprise party. I never knew what to expect. I would wake up to find the ward full of visitors or to find it completely empty, day or night.

One morning I awoke to an unfolding drama with the Patient across the aisle from me and one bed to the right. A nurse was frantically calling for assistance as she pushed on the man's chest. I don't know if it was simply time for me to wake up or if her calls for help woke me. In retrospect, I'd have preferred to remain sleeping.

Immediately, the room was filled with doctors and interns. A male doctor took over the pushing on the man's chest. Someone else inserted into his mouth a device attached to a large black rubber balloon which, when squeezed, would force air into his lungs. One young doctor called for someone to take notes on what was happening and the time it happened.

An orderly came into the ward, standing at my bed to watch the drama, ready to jump in if they needed his assistance. He was the one I'd taken to calling Senor Hernia, because he was the only person there who was large enough or strong enough to assist me out of bed into a wheelchair. Senor Hernia, who spoke a little English, told me that the female doctor in the group working on the man was his wife. It was she who took the longest needle I have ever seen for humans, curved and shiny, and inserted it to the hilt under one of the patient's nipples and injected a large quantity of fluid. None of their efforts seemed to make any difference. Even those paddles used in so many emergency room dramas didn't seem to work. The body didn't jump off the table in the way I'd been led to expect from watching too many hospital shows on television. Maybe the batteries were low.

I remember thinking that if I concentrated hard enough I might be able to see the man's soul leave his body, its brief ride on this earth completed for this round. I must not have tried hard enough for I saw nothing. Throughout the entire ordeal the man's wife/doctor remained professional and somewhat aloof. I did sense that all who played a part in this drama deferred to her throughout.

The drama completed, the body was left lying in the bed which was now somewhat askew, no longer in alignment with the others, having moved about quite freely during the action. The man's body, freshly bathed by the wash women and wrapped in the sheets of the bed, was lying on its back with only the face uncovered, like a newborn baby held up to the glass of the nursery window for all to witness the arrival of a new soul. Only this soul was leaving.

Everything I was watching seemed to occur in

compressed time, all in logical sequence but very rapid. The second act of this real life drama seemed to start without an intermission. An elderly woman, entering the ward flanked by two younger women, came to an abrupt halt when she saw the body, as if walking into an unseen barrier. She did so with a blink and a quick intake of breath, her head bouncing backward from the shock.

The younger women, oblivious to what had happened to her, continued on to the body, only then to realize what had happened. I learned later they were the man's sisters. They started crying loudly and asking the body's forgiveness for the mean things they had said and done to it while it was still functioning. At that moment I don't think the body really cared, but this was something the sisters needed, so the wailing continued for the appropriate amount of time for this group of survivors.

While the sisters were communing with their brother's dead body, a doctor asked the man in the bed next to it if he would like to be moved as the doctor was sure all of this had upset him.

"Nah," the man said. "I lived in New York for ten years. This is nothing new."

On that note, I hit a wall and became instantly tired, and went back to sleep terribly saddened. It was the first time I had seen anyone die up close.

When I awoke the bed was back in alignment, though empty. I too felt empty, my being somehow diminished by what had happened. I did not know the man, had never spoken to him. I had led a life I am sure was quite different from his. I had nothing in common with him other than that we were both traveling through this life on our own journeys and I missed him. Another lesson learned.

GOD WORKS IN MYSTERIOUS WAYS

One evening after our matronly cooks had collected the dishes from our latest feeding of beans and rice, a new inmate was added to our little group. An older man, very slight, so small in stature that you'd almost think he was an elf. He was carried in, lying on his side in the fetal position, strapped to a stretcher. He was crying great sobs that seemed to be coordinated with his convulsive shivering. The poor man must have been in great pain or scared out of his mind.

Senor Hernia appeared at my bedside to explain that the man was really not very ill, but was scared, this being his first visit to a hospital. As the orderlies placed the man in his bed he started reciting, loud enough for those in the next ward to hear, some sort of a poem. With my limited ability in the Spanish language I was unable to figure out what he was saying. Senor Hernia translated for me in his broken English: "Though I walk through the shadows of the valley of death..."

Now I really was in tune with the man's fear and, for some reason, this poor scared man's recital of the twenty-third psalm struck home with me. I had never attended church as an adult and, even as a child, only sporadically. But these words were familiar, and at that moment they really had meaning for me. This elf of a man was experiencing being close to death and was afraid of meeting it. I'd already met death but now I was also afraid. Not of death, for I no longer feared it, but of fear itself. Fear had always been a background noise in my life: fear of failure, which is a universal idea; fear of being a poor lover, shared by many adult men; fear of being a bad father to my children, shared by too few. But now this background noise had moved into the foreground and I did not like the feeling. It stayed with my semi-dysfunctional brain until the evening dose of medicine let me fall fitfully asleep.

Later that night I dreamed that the man was still reciting the twenty-third psalm though it seemed to be accompanied by a sporadic noise that was in unison with the recital. In my drug induced sleep I tried to ignore the words and accompanying noise but it soon overtook sleep and brought me awake. Both the recitation and the mystery sound were actually happening, though it took me some time to understand what exactly was going on. Our newest arrival was masturbating, his recital of the twenty-third psalm spoken in unison to his strokes, and he'd evidently been doing so for some time judging by the distress of the entire ward. Finally someone shouted for the nurses to get him to shut the fuck up. None of the female nurses wanted to go near the little man who'd turned from a helpless elf into a masturbating demon. I still didn't know what had brought him to the hospital but it was pretty clear it wasn't a problem with premature ejaculation. I drifted back to sleep thinking that this was my first experience of listening to a divinely inspired choking of the chicken.

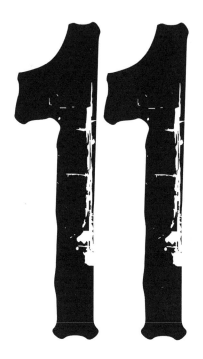

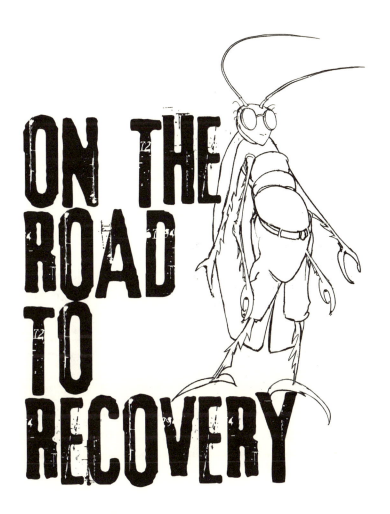

One of the benefits of undergoing a stroke is all the new adventures you get to take. In addition you get to take them after collecting years of experience. You don't really have to learn to walk all over again. You know that the object is to get from one spot to another, unlike the first time you learned to walk when it was all about the thrill and excitement of just being able to move upright instead of crawling. You just have to figure out how to get one leg to function. You know that if the leg once walked, it can walk again. All the parts are still there, you just have the adventure of finding out how to get them to work in harmony again. You also know that it will not happen overnight. It's going to take some time. I know that if I keep the desire to return to the way I once was as a priority, it will eventually happen. Every now and again the fear that it may not happen emerges, and you must fight to overcome the urge to give up.

Another benefit, or at least I think it a benefit, is that a stroke has the effect of peeling away years of socialization. You are given the chance to return to a more childlike state. My oldest son claims I have never left the childlike state where emotions are felt more deeply and occur quite rapidly. The filters of learned behavior are gone; you cry when you are sad and laugh when you are tickled. No occasion is inappropriate for these emotions even though your past experience tells you differently. I think this is why I was constantly falling in love with the women who nurtured me on this journey. Just love, not lust (well, maybe lust on a couple of occasions). A new and refreshing outlook on life. I loved everyone with whom I came in contact. A feeling of unity with others was a very comforting feeling. This could be a psychological survival ploy so you don't examine reality too closely or be overcome by the fear of failing to recover fully.

Despite this revelation of universal love, however, after about another week of it, I was ready to get the hell out of there. I'd experienced my first shower. Not that taking a shower was the motivating factor in my desiring release. I was just ready to get on with my life.

Senor Hernia had plopped me, naked, into a strange padded wheelchair and pushed me down the hall to the ward's latrine. There he helped me onto a toilet for my first big boy poop. Then back into the padded wheelchair and into a stall without a toilet, where he turned a hose of warm water on me. Another very attractive nurse then proceeded to soap me down. I did my own privates—a little difficult to do one-handed while sitting down on them. Then another dousing with warm water and the whole thing was over, except for the drying. Senor Hernia and the nurse wiped me off everywhere but my bottom, on which I was still sitting. Not to worry, Senor Hernia got me in a bear hug and held me upright while the nurse dried my ample bottom and not so ample privates. By now there was no modesty or sexual overtones to my nudity or having my banana dried off by a very attractive woman.

I explained to Senor Hernia that I again needed to sit on the toilet. Like a child trying out a new skill. While sitting there the attractive nurse in attendance opened the door to the stall and asked me if I sang.

While working my way through college, I had indeed sung for my supper. I sang in a folk group in a pizza restaurant on the weekends. We had a good college crowd following, so the gig continued for several years.

When I answered yes, the nurse asked me to sing for her. The latrine had tile walls. The dimensions of the room were such that my voice resonated very well, providing a nice quality to any sound I made, like singing in the shower. I tried to think of something she might know. The only thing I could think of was a song I had heard Julio Iglesias sing. So there I was, nude, sitting on a toilet, singing to an attractive woman, "*To all the girls I've loved before, who wandered in and out my door...*"

With that she let out a moan, clutched her breasts and ran from the room crying. I was either very, very good, or very, very bad. Senor Hernia helped me back into my padded wheelchair and said, with a sad but knowing smirk, "You sing very well."

That was the only singing gig I had while in the hospital. Probably the shortest and last in my singing carrier. I can no longer control the air from my lungs needed for singing, although I continually try.

Somewhere towards the end of my stay my ex-wife and son arrived. The wife first, sweeping in and taking charge. She was a take-charge kind of person. My security level went way up when I saw her. We had been married thirty years, most of which were good. It was only the last few that were stressful. I trusted her completely. I knew her and respected her even after all the hurt that we both felt from the end of our relationship. We had a thirty year history to go on. I felt that life was definitely going to get better now that she had arrived.

My son's arrival a day later caused a different kind of stir in the ward. Especially with the female staff. My son is handsome and a good sized boy. Six feet three inches, 250 pounds of well shaped body. Out of college, which he attended on a football scholarship, he was given a try out by one of our professional football teams. Even though he no longer played, he kept himself in good shape lifting weights and is an impressive specimen. When he arrived in the ward he was wearing lightweight cotton knit athletic shorts, a T-shirt and sneakers. The women members of the staff kept checking out his bottom, while the male members took note of his torso. Senor Hernia mentioned that he felt small now that he had seen my son. I tried to persuade him that he was equally impressive, which neither of us believed.

There were several conferences between my wife, James and the doctors to which I did not receive an invitation. The upshot was I could go home. Getting out of the hospital would prove more cumbersome than usual.

James, in an attempt to spare me the cost of the hospital stay as he knew I was flat broke, had told admissions that I was a *pensionado*, a retired person living in Costa Rica, and that I had the national medical insurance. Things started to get a bit sticky when the national insurance carrier could find no record of me. I was now an unclean person trying to scam the government. While I didn't really know what was wrong, I had learned that if it involved James he would somehow benefit at my expense. The good doctor insured me that there was no *problemo* whenever I would ask when I could leave. As far as he was concerned, there was no problem; I would just stay there until my bill was paid in cash, as I had now joined that part of society that lived on the fringes of honor. Something the hospital would no longer do with my credit card.

I had by now had enough of the place and wanted out. Another day was lost on the road to freedom, while my wife cashed a check at my Costa Rican bank to return to the hospital the next day with my bail in cash. Fourteen hundred dollars for almost a month of hospital stay.

Even when my day of departure finally arrived, it crept by endlessly and I felt that I would never leave. But the moment came. My son picked me up effortlessly and gently placed me in the wheelchair they'd rented for me, Senor Hernia standing by and watching in admiration.

The excitement of leaving for my own home left me abruptly. I was leaving the greatest source of loving people I had ever experienced. I was richer for the experience and saddened by my departure.

After a prolonged tour of the accounting department, I was finally pushed out into the bright sunlight of a glorious day. Like the day of my arrival it was warm, a soft breeze blowing and the sidewalk alive with fully functioning people rushing about. Normal activity again. I couldn't get enough of the scene and, trying to take it all in, I quickly reached overload. My mind slipped slightly out-of-sync with the information my eyes were sending it; I would see what was happening, but understood it only half a beat later, like watching a dubbed kung fu movie where the characters' lips move before the sound of their voice is heard. I quickly became tired.

Frustratingly, this mental lagging-behind would last for several weeks. I probably gave the appearance of being stupid, but I wasn't. I was just running slow.

The next several days turned out to be a time of emotional slow torture. Without asking for my input it was decided that instead of going to my home we would all stay at James's house and party. I am sure the rationale behind this was if I were to suffer another stroke I was in town closer to the clinic and doctors. I felt differently. I knew I was fine, albeit beaten up, and I wanted to get started learning how to operate in this new world of mine.

The thing I was most interested in was learning how to get out of bed and into my wheelchair. My agenda did not agree with that of those attending to me. I was held prisoner in James's guest house bed for a week. I was treated like an invalid, which I didn't feel I was. So an arm and a leg didn't work? So what? I was still the same feeling person I was before this mess occurred. These days were the worst part of my stroke continuum. Mentally I did not understand my body's new condition. Sometimes I still don't.

No mater what my protestations, my wife and son told me clearly I was wrong. They were staying in the main house. Every morning after breakfast with James and his wife my ex-wife and present son would show up at my bedside and dictate the new plan of attack. It became apparent to me that James was orchestrating the whole situation, which I resented because I didn't feel the decisions being made were in my best interest. It was decided that before I could go to my house the road would have to be repaired, so that an ambulance could make it up to my house in case I suffered another stroke. I reacted vehemently as I had recently paid to have the road smoothed out.

Next it was decided that my son needed a Costa Rican power of attorney in case something were to happen. Jesus, I thought, these people are planning for my death not my recovery. All of these decisions were handed down from on high with overtones of arrogance which hurt me to this day. I soon realized that what would happen would happen and became silent, which I am sure was taken as a turn for the worse.

After I returned to my house on the mountain things got back to normal, except for the time I caught James with my bank book in his pocket. It turned out that the committee had made several trips to my house to decide what could be done to make it livable for an invalid, a state I had yet to accept. The result of their visits was to have hand rails installed next to my bed and in the bathroom next to the shower and toilet. During these visits, my ex-wife later told me, James would read my diary until she would take it away from him and tell him it was none of his business.

The unfortunate thing about it all was that my ex

and my son bought into James's agenda. If they had just stopped to ask themselves why they'd made the sacrifice to leave job and family and come to Cost Rica, which I know was out of love and concern for me and a desire to help, this may not have happened. But, like any good sales representative, James had thrown enough Good Samaritan deeds into the mix to make everything that happened seem to be part of the common goal of saving my life. Even today James tells all those who are not familiar with my little midlife speed bump that if it had not been for his heroic efforts I would have died. True, true, true. Maybe.

The two greatest expenditures of money were for the road repair—unnecessary in my opinion; an ambulance had fetched me off the mountain once, it could do it again—and the hiring of a new Costa Rican lawyer to review the status of my land purchase and draw up a power of attorney for my son to take over my affairs in Costa Rica. This accomplished nothing in helping me get better. It did however piss off my attorney that had worked faithfully for me for several years and generate new attorney's fees. All that money could have gone toward physical therapy. My savior James had other motivations than simply helping my recovery. He collected commissions from the road company and possibly the attorney.

Shortly after I had been left to my own devices, in my own home, with my ex and my son now back in the States, James showed up to inform me that he had arranged for me to be admitted to a "nursing home" in town. Hell, I didn't even know we had a nursing home.

Now the new plan of attack was for me to agree to be committed to an institution where according to James I would be taken care of. My cognition had been rapidly catching up with my surroundings but, even in my now somewhat less slow state, I didn't understand. James had explained his effort to find someone to take care of me in my own home as something marginally less than Homeric. If this was true why did he expend so much effort if the goal was to have me committed?

Because of my fragile and admittedly somewhat paranoid mental state, this all smelled very bad to me. It was difficult following his rationale for this move. Even with all the sales pitches he threw at me there didn't seem to be any logical reason to do as he wished. When I rejected his invitation he left abruptly and seemingly very frustrated, dismissing me with a wave of his hand and a dismissive turn away from me. It was like I wasn't worth his time or was of a lesser status. I didn't see the need for such behavior under the circumstances.

Several weeks before my stroke, James had proudly told me how he had worked a deal with an international real estate company to be their "consultant" for the part of Costa Rica in which we lived. He would "advise" potential Real Estate purchasers regarding property in our area. For this valuable advice he would receive a good percentage of the sales price as a commission for his efforts. I didn't doubt the business relationship, only the amount of commission he claimed he would receive. This was standard operating procedure for James, always describing any event in which he took part in the way most flattering to him. His ego was even larger than his ample belly.

Originally, when first placed under house arrest in James's guest house, I had tried to get those who loved me, and were there to help me, to just get me back to my house. But I was too slow mentally to be able to express myself logically. In the end it all boiled down to my efforts sounding like misdirected anger. I really didn't know what James was up to, but I instinctively knew that all the activity was not for my benefit but for his. Later, after the shouting and the tumult had died down, Nidia, my recently acquired cleaning lady, cook and nurse, told me that James was planning on buying my farm because he had a buyer lined up for it. That hurt a lot. If it was true, James looked at me not as a friend but as a source of income. He was rooting for my death and had arranged the legal niceties so he could end up with my farm for his personal benefit. This was not my only rude revelation on my new life's journey, merely the first.

The road repair and title search now made an unpleasant kind of sense to me. They did nothing to help me get better, but they did pave the way for a potential sale of my farm. Since the day James visited me to try to have me volunteer to be committed into an institution from which I didn't know that I could have effected my own release, he has never been back to visit me. I can only guess that he feels that I have completely recovered and no longer need his companionship or that he is very busy selling real estate for the big international real estate company.

Whatever our friendship had been, it was not, for me at least, strong enough to survive my recognition of the lack of integrity James displayed in all this. It's funny; I thought my feeling of loss would be significantly greater than it is, but I see that all along I'd been approaching our friendship on a level much different than he had. We were, after all, just drinking buddies. He was right, I was wrong. I should have seen him that way. Just someone to get drunk with, to enjoy while drunk, but in the bare light of a sober day not someone you should trust.

I miss him. We used to have so much fun.

12

PRACTICE PRACTICE PRACTICE

I stayed at my house for over a month before I could return to the States where I hoped to get therapy to learn to walk and to talk like a big boy. My days at home quickly developed into a routine.

I had been discharged from the hospital with enough medicine to last me until well after I could return to the States. Every morning just after sunrise, Joel my night watchman would show up to help me dress and host the ceremony of the pills. My God, I take a lot of the things. I have gotten so I have progressed from choking on a piece of bread to the point were I now down seven or eight pills in one glorious swallow.

The process of dressing me was that I would sit on the edge of the bed while Joel scooted my underwear and pants up my legs as far as they would go, and then I'd grab one of the many hand rails installed for my survival and stand up so that everything could be pulled up to their final resting place and secured. We would hold our collective breath for the transfer to the rented wheelchair. Most of the time it worked.

I only got into trouble when I would try something that to my recollection and imprinting was just a simple movement. Things were not as they used to be and I would end up on the floor. A view I would become used to during the ensuing month. For, once down, I had neither the strength nor the training to get my lard ass off the floor and back into my wheelchair. On several occasions I spent the better part of the day hanging out on the floor studying the local insect life before I was able to get anyone's attention. A regular sized Costa Rican could not lift me but I figured out a way a Good Samaritan could slide a board under my butt, which I could get off the ground a few inches using my right arm to roll first away from the board then roll onto it bottom down. We'd slide a cement block under the board creating a lever, and then all that was needed was for my rescuer to stand on the other end of the board, like a teeter totter, to lift my bottom high enough that I was able to use the wheelchair to steady my ascent and lift myself into it.

Anyway, the day would start when Joel and I would share the Pill ceremony, some coffee, and some toast, after which he'd take off for his daily routine of watering all the new plants I had installed before I hit this little speed bump in my life. Joel had a unique way of having his buttered toast. He would take the two pieces of hot toast fresh from the toaster, place a large blob of butter in the center of one of the pieces, and then smack the other dry piece on top to make a toast sandwich. Different strokes for different folks.

About mid-morning my own private angel would show up to take over. Nidia had been interviewed by my ex and approved for consumption by the committee. An unmarried woman of about forty, short (she just about reached my arm pit), and full of life and genuine compassion. She is still in my life today and will be for a long long time. I owe her a debt that can never be repaid. Her nature is so good that she doesn't even comprehend that a debt of gratitude is involved.

She has at least three children all with the benefit of no husband involved. As she explained one day; "Yo sin niño, yo en mucho fiestas tomar mucho, yo con noveo stomaco grande, no mas noveo." I without children in many parties, drink a lot, with my boyfriend, stomach large, no more boyfriend. The last part of this declaration was accompanied by gestures indicating a pregnant stomach and a slap of the hands in a sliding motion to indicate the departure of her lover.

No sorrow and most importantly no shame. I have met two of her children. They are beautiful people obviously well loved. When there was no school she would bring them with her up to my house.

She was like my mother, feeding me, dressing me, bathing me, putting me on the potty. Having another person undo your pants and pull them down so you could sit on the toilet took some getting used to, especially when the other person is a *tica* with a wicked sense of humor. Every time, as I would stand in front of the toilet using my one working hand to hold on to a handrail, Nidia would undo my belt, then the zipper on my fly, then reach around me and pull down both my pants and underwear with one quick expert motion, all the while muttering "*practica, practica, practica*." Practice, practice, practice.

What a great attitude toward her journey through life.

I slowly made some improvement. José had arranged for me to get some therapy at the hospital in Cartago. Once a week, the three of us would take off in his taxi for my therapy. My therapist was about as old as I was, a kind woman who really knew her stuff. On first arriving at the hospital she would check me out, gauging my ability to move my left leg. Nidia would explain that I moved my left leg with my right leg or my bad arm with my good arm. Pleased with this report, the therapist would move to my arm, flicking the fingers and pounding on the biceps to encourage movement. She could sense muscle contraction or perceive any movement, no matter how faint, when I could feel nothing.

Under these circumstances—when your body is trying to reestablish nerve paths or establish new ones to your muscles—your attempt to move a finger results in a whole body response. Everything is tightened in an attempt to get through to the offending member. While all of this is actually happening, it seems like a terribly frustrating and tiring exercise in futility and about an hour of it was all I could take.

I've never become discouraged with my progress, no matter how small, for wonderful little surprises were occurring, especially in that half-awake state in the morning when fully rested but not quite fully conscious. I would find that my arm would move without conscious thought. Or my leg would do some little thing it was unable to do the day before. On the outside it didn't look like anything was happening, on the inside great strides were taking place.

I looked forward to these weekly trips for I was getting cabin fever staying at home.

Two to three weeks before my scheduled departure for the States, I decided that next week I would walk. I didn't know if I could, I just felt it was time. The following week, after being placed on the therapy type bed, I pushed myself upright and, using the four footed cane I had bought several weeks earlier, I took my first couple of steps in over a month. I was scared and shaking as I did so but those feelings were drowned out by happiness and pride. I could walk. I wouldn't be bound to a wheelchair. The world was truly wonderful again. Oh boy, if I only knew.

In truth, I really didn't take steps. I swung my left foot forward by lifting my hip until the leg cleared the floor then twisted my hips, throwing the whole leg in front of me. Awkward, but effective. And all I was able to do at the time. It did more for my psyche than my physical recovery. I would grab any sign of progress no matter how small and cherish the moment. That would help keep me going.

A wheelchair takes some getting used to. First, they're very good at placing your bottom on the floor if the brakes aren't set. Second, they provide a new outlook on life. Literally. Your eyes seem to be at the universal height for women's breasts. Costa Rican women dress for men, not for women. Wow! Doing the mall populated by these lovely creatures was another reason to live. Maybe sometime in the future. Every thing was possible in the future.

After my therapy sessions, José, Nidia and I would go shopping in Cartago, where there was a good sized supermarket. Nidia would push me down the aisles, loading up my lap with our week's worth of food. All of this would quickly become unbearably painful. While utilitarian, a wheelchair is not a comfortable chair. Your basic model comes with no padding and, as I was still experiencing leg spasms and pain, I didn't need prolonged time in a wheelchair to help the process of pain accumulation. In addition, I would still often become suddenly exhausted. When this occurred, I would become light-headed and afraid. So, uncomfortable as it was, the wheelchair was a necessity for the times during shopping when I would pass out.

Overall these outings were food for my soul. It was if seeing the happy people, the magnificent women, the children, reaffirmed to me that I was still part of the human experience. That there was a higher meaning to us. I might make it despite the odds.

As the day for my return to the states drew closer I became more fearful. I was concerned that in my new condition I wouldn't be able to handle the real world. Whenever I had ventured out of my house up until then, it had been under the very strong protection of José and Nidia.

It didn't help matters much that, when I called American Airlines to confirm my reservation and ask that they provide a wheelchair, the person I was talking to asked abruptly, "You can walk to the plane, can't you?"

I didn't know that this was asked in order that the airline could make a wheelchair available. I heard it instead as a very clear message that if I couldn't walk to the plane, I wouldn't fly. In addition, the person sharply told me that I would be required to show a doctor's certificate indicating that I was well enough to fly. Welcome back to the real world. There were some brief moments when I would have happily said screw it, I'm staying. But the other urge was stronger, the urge to return to the States, where at least I would be able to understand most of what was being said around me.

The day before my departure, Nidia loaded up my pantry with all my valuables that were going to stay for my return. My house is remote and Costa Rica is a poor country, and a gringo's house left unoccupied is an open invitation to anyone who cared to do a little out of season Christmas shopping. So, in designing my house, I had it built with a very large pantry completely out of reinforced concrete. Top, bottom, front, back, everything. The door is metal with three locks. My furniture is built out of concrete. The couches, the bed frame, my kitchen, all concrete. All of my appliances are on rollers so that whenever I return to the States everything can be moved into the pantry. My house has been broken into four times while I was away but, in each instance, nothing was taken because there was nothing they could take. My hope was that the bad guys would get the message and find easier pickings. Before leaving this time, I wondered if maybe I should leave a note on my door telling them that the other gringo, James, is much more wealthy than me and never at home as he's always out selling real estate.

The day of my departure, José arrived at my house at five AM. We put the bedclothes in the pantry and locked it up. The ride to the airport over the roads I had recently traveled so much, both horizontally and vertically, was a poignant trip to take. While I knew that there was family waiting for me in the States who were very worried about me, I didn't want to go. I was scared and frightened about what unforeseen calamity could be waiting for me, but it was time to return to my other home.

The airport was the expected zoo. José had to go and fetch a wheelchair for me. I had never traveled on an airline as a person needing a wheelchair before. This was a new and refreshing experience. The guy that was assigned to wheeling me about was cheerful and gregarious. I tried to explain to the nice woman at the check in counter that I didn't fit in the seats and that I needed to be able to straighten out my left leg. She handled my request with the learned politeness that we all have encountered. All airline personnel must go through training on how to politely handle complaints when the real message they convey is, "Tough shit, you will take what I give you."

I was given an aisle seat in the rear of the plane on the left side where the injured leg would be held captive. Away from a seat on my right that my good arm needed to leverage myself up and out of the seat in which I sat.

This was the only time I was disillusioned with their service, other than the time I read a message from the Chairman and CEO in the airline magazine in which he said that American Airlines provided the legroom the American flying public wanted. Accompanying the article was a picture of an individual—I assume the author of the piece—who looked to be vertically challenged and only flew first class anyway, so what the hell would he know about legroom? Many months later I saw him interviewed on television on his retirement, smiling proudly when he acknowledged that he had saved the airline hundreds of thousands of dollars a year by removing olives from the salads served with in-flight meals. I still have difficulty with this approach to business.

Since the stroke, I hadn't really walked in any real-life situations. Only during my therapy sessions, which was like staying in the safety of the shallow end of the swimming pool when you first learn to swim. So boarding the plane was my first real-life solo. Because of the cane, and my bulk, I was forced to crab-walk sideways down the aisle. I was accompanied by a concerned flight attendant who either literally didn't hear what I was saying about not fitting in their seats or just didn't want to deal with it.

On the way down the aisle, my left arm took off on its own. You would think that an arm without muscle control would just hang at your side obediently. They don't. They go where the tendons let them go which may or may not be at your side. My left arm decided that, while my body traversed the aisle, it would visit all those sitting on the right side aisle seats. Those passengers who were not watching were slapped in the head by it. A petite little old lady had her large strawberry colored bouffant hairdo destroyed with one awkward swipe. I really do know how to make friends quickly, don't I?

On reaching my seat—32c, situated away from an armrest for my one good arm—I was unable to descend slowly and I ended up painfully wedged into it. The pain increased the entire flight. By the time we reached Miami, I was crying. My seat-mates, as well as those around me who had heard me explain my condition and describe the pain I was in, were ready to lynch the first American employee they saw.

When it came to my turn to exit the plane on arrival in Miami, I was unable to get out of the seat with one arm. I probably couldn't have done it before the stroke either. The little old lady and her husband sitting inside me had to climb over the seats in front. It took three men to extract me from my painful seat. When the first lad arrived he asked softly and politely, "What seems to be the problem here?"

I responded softly and politely, "I don't fit in your FUCKING seats."

Enough said. He understood immediately. Evidently the passengers sitting around me let their feelings be known about how American Airlines treated stroke victims as they reached the counter at the gate. A small wheelchair that fit in the center aisle was brought on board. I was extracted from my seat, during which my left arm was pulled from the shoulder socket. It has taken over a year to get my left shoulder to stay in the socket. I tried to warn those trying to help that my arm was fragile, but one look at my bulk apparently convinced them otherwise. Now I literally hurt all over.

My bottom was about two inches wider than the skinny wheelchair, and my left arm kept leaving my lap so it could wedge itself between the chair and an aisle seat. Trying to hold it against my chest with my right arm so it wouldn't get caught made the shoulder sting. We had to back up several times to free me.

On the next leg of our journey, I was upgraded to first class where I fit, but can't afford. I slept most of the way to Dallas, where I'd have to change planes again. When we landed, I was almost run over by passengers eager to get off the plane. I just made it to the waiting wheelchair without falling. At this stage of my little journey to recovery, the floor was always moving up and down when I stood, so falling would be the next trick I would need to master. The more fatigued I became, the more the floor would move. I was placed onto one of those electric carts with other infirm or lazy individuals and off we went to the next gate. The cart stopped some twenty yards away from the gate. Evidently the driver assumed that I would walk the distance but, when I almost fell on my face trying to get out of the cart, his attitude quickly changed. Luckily for me there was a wheelchair at the gate for a departing passenger. I guess part of the airline training does not include the concept that when a person requests a wheelchair that means for the entire period he or she is in the terminal waiting for a plane. The person who met me figured their job was finished when I was placed on the electric cart. Someone should have phoned ahead to have a wheelchair waiting when the cart got there.

In Dallas I was given the right side aisle bulkhead seat that I had requested six months earlier when I traveled to Costa Rica. My bottom was in coach, my feet in first class. I spent the majority of this last leg to Seattle sleeping.

My arrival in Seattle where my son, his wife and my brand new grandson lived was almost as emotionally intense as my arrival in the states after my three year tour of duty in Africa. Like then, I felt the impact of the less than normal life I had been living flush out of my system all at once. I was finally back in the States. At that moment, for me at least, Miami and Dallas qualified as third world countries.

I remember asking the person who pushed me up the ramp if I would have a wheelchair to get to baggage claim. He told me, "I'm sure of it. There is a great big guy with a wheelchair waiting for you."

When we made it to the passenger waiting area, the great big guy turned out to be my son. In his Seattle summer weekend uniform of shorts, T-shirt, and sneakers, he looked about as good to me as he did the first time I ever saw him.

"Hi, Dad," he said. "You look great. How you doing?"

Throwing his arms around me, he picked me up, placed me gently in the wheelchair he'd brought to the gate, and off we went. I felt like I was still flying. He was just walking at his normal speed but, to me, it seemed to be three times faster than anything I had experienced in the past months.

"Jesus, slow down," I said. "You're scaring the hell out of me."

"Don't be a sissy, Dad. We're not going fast at all."

I would get used to his gentle scolding during the next several months as he continued to encourage me to do better with my recovery. God, I love him.

We collected my luggage, which consisted of two very large plastic storage containers filled with as many packages of coffee as I could afford. They make nice presents. I always make sure to take down the name of the person who gets me my seat and checks me in. Then when I go down to Costa Rica again I bring them a package of coffee as thanks. Maybe someday I'll send a package to the retired Chairman and CEO of American. He may not know jack shit about legroom other than what some bean counter tells him, but he does know how to run one hell of a good airline.

My son deposited me and my two little plastic crates at the curb while he went to get the car. It was cold, many headlights and tail lights sparkling in the damp street as cars jockeyed for a position close to the curb in a way that would assure their being able to get out. As I sat watching all this I realized that getting out was an unrealistic expectation. It was fun, sort of like watching a clown act at the circus. Except that this car dancing was not rehearsed, but impromptu. Costa Ricans do it much better.

After a short wait my son arrived, threw the trunks in the back and me in the passenger seat, and off we went. I was very uneasy with his driving. Something was seriously wrong. Then it hit me. He was driving in a straight line. He wasn't swerving to avoid the potholes, as there were none. A very uncomfortable feeling.

He lives in West Seattle with a view of Puget Sound to the West. We parked in the alley as it was downhill to his house. I had never done steps before and on the ride in we'd decided that going down steps would probably be easier than going up steps.

With him holding me, we made it to the house and down the outside steps to the basement, where the door was opened by a very concerned daughter in law. My son deserves the best life has to offer and when this lady agreed to marry him the best is exactly what he got. If I had a daughter, I would want her to be exactly like my son's wife. She is also very lippy.

"Okay, mister," she said. "What the hell do you mean, scaring the hell out of all of us?"

"Hi," I said. "I'm glad to see you too."

We all spent the next couple of hours catching up and admiring the new life with which we were all so recently blessed; my grandson. My God, they grow quickly. In the six months I had been gone, my grandson had sprouted. No longer that little bundle who would take a morning nap with me, lying on my chest in peaceful sleep, now he could really move about. I am sure he broke no crawling speed records, but one moment he was there, the next, empty space. It was sure fun watching my son—who had cheerfully done the same thing to me as a child—get his, so to speak.

My room was in the basement, a hallway removed from the bathroom and the big screen TV, my closest companion for the next few weeks. Since his visit to Costa Rica, my son had spent a great deal of time trying to get the Veterans Administration to agree to admit me to a facility for treatment and therapy.

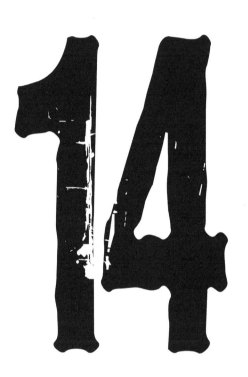

In business for myself, I was, like so many independent businessmen, without health insurance. The premiums were onerous and the benefits minimal. The Hospital care promised to me when I enlisted during the Korean War was the only thing that I had.

Something had happened since those simpler times of the fifties. The US had changed. It was no longer Donna Reed and Father Knows Best but in your face screw you Bart Simpson that were our present role models. Both in society and congress. Our elected officials were now, as Joel would say, *cope nalgus.* A cooperative of assholes.

They felt no obligation to fulfill the contract made with us years earlier when our government, right or wrong, needed our bodies. The Veterans Administration was suffering the budget cuts promised by the newest political pundit, an obnoxious fat little man named Newt who had never been in the service and whose moral standards were so high that he had to be taken to court by his ex-wife to get him to pay child support. I would love for Newt baby to be in my situation instead of getting free hospital care for the rest of his life paid by others. Enough of this political BS. Things are as things are. If you don't like it, get the hell out. Which, thank God, I can do. I will always get to pay my taxes though.

My son had become very frustrated in trying to get a straight answer from the VA. Most of the representatives he had talked to provided illogical answers to his questions. The sad thing is that these people had all become so acclimated to the bureaucratic bullshit that their answers *were* logical. To them. On a whole, I think those administrative people are lucky as they most probably could not make it in the real world.

I had arrived on a Friday, and the next morning we began our quest to get me admitted to a VA hospital. We went to the Pacific Medical Center, where we believed we had been instructed to go. It certainly looked like a VA hospital. The buildings were of brick, the grounds well kept. It was the place my son had gone to when he was recruited out of high school to play football at the air force academy. He chose the University of Idaho, close to where his girlfriend at the time went to school. There was a sign at the clinic entrance indicating that the place was shut down for the weekend, and that persons needing treatment should go to Swedish Hospital. Which we did.

There was some confusion as to my status at Swedish but we were now dealing with bright, thinking administrative types whose primary mission was to provide medical care and not to worry about doing anything that could get them into trouble. Besides, they didn't need to worry about if I could pay or not because that was a problem for the accounting department. Hospital bills are now one of, if not the, leading cause of personal bankruptcy filings in the U.S. There, but for the grace of the VA, go I.

I was quickly placed on one of those emergency room beds and plugged into many electronic monitoring devices, even though I told them I had no insurance and could not pay the bill. These people didn't care. They wanted to help me. My son and I were both greatly relieved. Finally some action was taking place. My emergency room doctor was female and gave me the feeling that she was competent. I felt comfortable with her attending me. Another "bat can" was ordered so onto a gurney and off we went, down hallways and up elevators. The place seemed to be immense.

It is funny the things you remember in stressful situations. Nonsensical things stay with you. I remember that the woman who ran the Swedish hospital "bat can" machine had the greatest ass I had ever seen, far surpassing the trophy asses pointed out by James in Costa Rica. In addition she wore tight jeans to make sure admiring males could tell. The rest of her was also very pleasing to the eyes of a practicing dirty old single man. Getting me onto the carriage that moved in and out of the huge metal donut that bombarded my skull with magical rays proved to be a bit difficult. It moved, I didn't. I then understood why the operator dressed as she did. It wasn't to give dirty old men a thrill, it was so she could climb up onto the apparatus and, like my first ambulance driver the night of my stroke, scoot me into place. Only she didn't fart and smelled one hell of a lot better than my driver.

I was next taken to X-ray to have my left knee and hip X-rayed. Ever since my flight to the States on the airline that provided the American flying public the legroom they wanted, my left hip and knee hurt like hell. After that it was back to the emergency room to get plugged in again and await the results of the machines.

In due course the results were in and to the surprise of no-one it was discovered that I had suffered a fairly good CVA. Whatever the hell that was, it meant stroke.

Toward the end of our visit we found out that we had originally gone to the wrong facility. We were given directions to the real VA hospital, which was miles from where we had started.

On Monday morning my son took off from his new job to take me to the right hospital as we were sure that it would not accept new patients on a Sunday. He had only been with his new company a few weeks so to take time off was quite stressful for him. He wanted his new employer to feel good about their decision to hire him. Now he was forced to take time from his job to care for his father. That included taking time to come home in the morning to help me on and off the toilet. So one of the first things I learned was to time my morning duty to coincide with my son's midmorning coffee break. From there I graduated to getting on and off the toilet all by myself.

My brother, who has been crippled with rheumatoid arthritis since he was twenty-eight, is also a veteran. He has been in the VA system for years. He had been telling my son to drive to the emergency entrance of the hospital, push me out of the car, and leave. It is his opinion that the only way to effectively deal with the administrative bullshit of the VA is not to give them any options. My son thought my brother was just joking. My brother's approach became more valid as we spent the entire day getting the runaround.

Even those organizations populated by an overabundance of cretins have some hidden gems who get things done. The first hidden gem that I found was "Eligibility, front desk Joe." Eligibility sat at the admitting desk simultaneously answering the phone and admitting those who appeared before him. He did this for hours on end without a break and without losing his professionalism. I really don't know his name other than it must be Joe. He greeted me cheerfully when my turn in the barrel came up. His attitude seemed to be that a veteran was sitting in front of him and it was his job to get him admitted to the hospital. I would soon find bureaucratic assholes whose goal was to keep you from being admitted. As I started the admissions process, my son left me to return to work. I waited the entire day to see a doctor for an evaluation. In the end I never did see a doctor, just a medic. By the time my evaluation could take place my son was able to rejoin me.

This little slimeball medic ushered us into a small examining room and started to stick pins in me to check reflexes. Evidently he thought I was faking it as he told us there was nothing the VA could do for me because I had already had my stroke. Apparently the only way this jerk would admit me was if I had a stroke and passed out in his presence. He then proceeded to lecture my son on how he had taken care of his own father until his father had died and implied that my son should do the same. The consummate insult from someone neither socially nor mentally up to my son's level. The bureaucratic battle was joined. Though polite, it was clear my son and I were not leaving until presented with other options. The option we chose was to see a rehabilitation doctor in one week. The first open appointment.

For the week I was confined to the basement to enjoy daytime TV on the big screen there was only one serious mishap. One night after being tucked in to bed an outside light was shining through the window because the shade was up. I got out of bed and slowly made my way over to the window. There was a table directly under the window which I had to circumnavigate to pull down the shade. Pulling down the shade caused me to lose my balance and drop onto the table first then the floor. I ended up with a severe bruise on my left side bracketed by large patches that no longer had the epidermal layer of skin for protection. In other words I was a bloody mess. After he got me off the floor, my son bawled me out for wandering about in the dark. Mostly it was his frustration at not being able to get me help that surfaced.

In the week before our next scheduled appointment I called my brother for advice.

"Look out for the assholes," he counseled. "They are the ones that to say yes means that they will have to do some work. Do not take no for an answer. Threaten to go over their head if you have to, but don't give up. Your goal is to get into the system. Once in the system, it will take care of you."

What the hell did that mean, "The system will take care of you?"

The next week two very determined gentlemen went to the hospital. My son had contacted his Congressman and was about to drop a very big political hammer on the local VA. I again felt like hell. Again everything to the left hurt. As it turned out, there was no need for our determination because this time we met only gems, those that could do something. The first doctor took less than five minutes to examine me and my new wound, and then excused himself for a minute. He returned with the head of Rehabilitative Services, who took an equally brief look see and said, "I am admitting you right now."

"Ugh, can I go home and get some clothes?" I said.

"No."

I was now in the system.

FAST, FAST, FAST, TILL THE THRILL OF SPEED OVERCOMES THE FEAR OF DEATH

"Jackson, you lard ass. What are you doing in bed? You were due in X-ray twenty minutes ago."

It was Angie, the floor nurse, who less than three minutes ago had greeted me on my first arrival on Five East. A stocky Italian woman with red curly hair, she was originally from New Jersey, and I liked her immediately as she was lippy, a trait most honorable to me. Within seconds we were giving each other a bad time and enjoying it.

Swedish Hospital was a one room school house compared to this place. It went on forever. Within a minute of being told I was being admitted, a slight oriental woman twice my age showed up to plop me into a wheelchair and push me to what was to be my new home for the next month or so. I was embarrassed to have her pushing me as I was three times her size and weight. Some weeks later, while taking Physical therapy, I met this same wonderful woman. She had just pushed Mr. Watanabe, another stroke victim, into therapy. The two of them made a beautiful couple, both in the latter years of their life, both the picture of health. When I asked her if Mr. Watanabe was her boyfriend she replied, "Oh no, he's too young. He is only 83." Please God let me find a woman like her when I am only 83.

At our first meeting Angie quickly pushed me into a four bed ward complete with its own bathroom and introduced me to my new room mates.

"This is Bracken, Morin and DuPont," she said. "Watch out for those two." She gestured toward Morin and DuPont, both of whom had assumed the most innocent look they could muster for our initial meeting.

"Those two are the biggest collection of gold bricks I have ever met," Angie said, "and they can't leave soon enough for me."

All of this meant she liked them.

They both said hi, or something suitable. Bracken didn't say a word, just looked at me with a blank look. Bracken looked at everybody and everything with a blank look. His stroke had affected him much more than mine had me. Oh joy.

"What the hell do you mean I was due in X-ray twenty minutes ago?" I said. "I just got here."

"That's no excuse," she said. "Let's go."

She threw off my bed covers and moved the wheelchair closer to the bed. I was out of the room before I even had a chance to talk with my new room mates.

The X-ray department took pictures of my hip and my knee again, as well as a couple covering the area I'd hit on falling, which was now a multicolored blotch of yellow, brown and blue.

On returning to my room I met my new doctor.

"Hi, I'm Larry Brown," he said. "I'm your internist." He was a young Asian man with a great smile. "How you doing?" he asked. "Having trouble staying upright, I see. Why you fall down and go boom?"

"It seemed like a good idea at the time," I replied.

"Mind if I take a look at you?" he said, starting without waiting for my assent. He looked in my eyes, at my arm, my leg, my stomach. Then came the smacking and sticking. Smack one knee with the rubber mallet and watch both legs jerk. Try the left elbow, that was so much fun.

Whack.
Nothing.
Oh boy, this could take awhile.

Before he could finish, a group of doctors showed up and the tallest one came forward, stuck out his hand, and told me he was doctor so and so, my neurologist. I now had an internist and neurologist on my staff. I could hardly wait to find out what was next.

Neurologist is the Latin word for pin sticker. I got the sharp end of a pin stuck in most parts of my anatomy. They kept showing up until well after five. Not good looking women with magnificent breasts, but doctors. It was a surreal type of experience; doctors and specialists by the truck load coming by for a visit, the neurologist twice. The party also included the dietitian, who would make sure I didn't choke on my food. Being "in the system" was a bit overwhelming.

Things really didn't slow down to a routine I could handle for over a week. When they did it was only because all the doctors knew what was wrong with me and had set about making me right again.

Every doctor or team of doctors needed a test taken on me. There were technicians from the lab who would draw blood for the various tests. They were very good at what they did, taking their required vials of blood almost painlessly. As a child, my first needle shot ended badly. The needle broke off in my arm. That was so long ago, back when needles were used over and over, being sterilized in an autoclave between uses so they wouldn't infect the next person. I still do not like needles.

I was sent to a lab one floor down for an ultra sound, something I had never gone through before. It was all computer graphics to me. I had spent almost thirty years in the computer industry, so I became interested in what was going on. The technician knew her business and explained what she was doing in a clear logical manner that was easy to follow. I was doing okay with all of her instructions until she told me to lie still and not talk. She then started moving her little wand over my neck, all the while asking me questions about Costa Rica.

"How am I supposed not to talk if you're going to keep asking me questions all the time?" I said.

"Just shut up and pretend you're a husband."

That I understood.

She was the one that expanded the doctor's request and discovered that the artery going up the right side of my neck supplying the right half of my brain with blood was one hundred percent blocked. The left side was only forty percent blocked.

It didn't take a mental giant to understand the severity of this observation. With only half a brain getting sixty percent of the blood it should, I knew a severe lifestyle modification was in the works.

"How come I'm not dead?" I asked.

I received an explanation on how the body protects the brain, and goes about repairing it when damaged. How the brain grows new little blood vessels to supply the part that is deficient. I was now getting my supply of brain blood from my left side artery and up the back of my neck. I was impressed with what the body can do to protect the brain. When she was through I felt a little less concerned and a great relief that I was one of the animals she had just described. I took her one of my packages of coffee a few days later.

The morning of the day after I was admitted started rapidly. I had not yet finished my breakfast when Angie started my day off right.

"Hurry up, lard ass. You're late for PT."

"What's PT?" I asked.

"Pain and torture. You'll love it. Get moving."

Morin and DuPont chimed in. "Yeah, get moving, lard ass. You're going to love it." Almost in unison. They were a real pair to draw to. Bracken didn't say a word. He just stared blankly.

Off I went to meet my mistress of Pain and Torture. Her name was Beverly, a beautiful black woman with a refined aura about her.

She started me on my way to walking like a normal human being again by placing me on a low workout table and having me move my left leg as much as I could. Which turned out to be very little.

I was lucky to be assigned to her as a Patient. The positive attitude of this group of therapists kept pain and torture an upbeat place to be. They even had music playing on a radio to help with the upbeat mood of the place. No mater how many times I asked, they could not find a radio station playing my favorite banana song.

Occupational Therapy, next door to physical therapy, was much different. No music and rather sterile.

When I first started PT I could only work for a few minutes before I would get tired and have to quit.

I would spend more time being pushed to PT by one of the many wonderful volunteers at the hospital than I would working out. I couldn't tell, but there was progress being made.

Even today, getting tired is something I never have been able to get used to. I am not talking about normal tiredness that comes after exercise or a long day of work. This stuff is much more potent. It hits you without warning and its effects are debilitating. If you are standing when it hits, you can no longer stand. Even today I must lie down several times a day to counteract this quick and sudden tiredness. Actually, tiredness isn't a strong enough word. Exhaustion fits the mood much better.

I am by nature a very impulsive individual. I want to do things now, not a minute from now, not a day from now, but right now. I am sure God put this little speed bump in my life to force me to slow down and enjoy the rest of it but my standard outlook was still with me when I started therapy. My attitude was, "a couple of days of this shit and I'm out of here." Now I've learned better. I make these types of plans for years, not days.

Initially, there was a great deal of internal frustration that things were not going as fast as they normally would. At night when the TV sets, hanging from the ceiling of our four bed ward, had finally grown silent and sleep wouldn't visit me, I would recall the condition I was in when first admitted into the system and try to recognize just how much progress we had made to date. This would keep me going. It was only by looking at the larger picture that I could tell there was some progress being made. As I learned to live with my condition, I also learned how to identify the small gains when they were made. This helped in coming to grips with what had happened to me. Because of this approach I never went through any of the "what did I do to deserve this" type attitude.

Another emotion, however, surfaced alongside my acceptance of what had happened to me. A counterpoint to the positive approach to which I naturally migrated. Fear. In those wee hours where sleep evaded me, I started to be afraid of my uncertain future. Could I, would I, be able to live in the world I knew as I had before? Just a slight background nagging, the flipside to my optimistic outlook.

Despite the simmering fear, though, my intent was to overcome this new challenge, radically different to any I'd previously encountered. I was very lucky in this regard. I met several inmates who were angry, full of self pity because they couldn't find a reason that they'd been hit with a stroke. Sometimes there is no reason, stuff just happens. On a different level, I believe this is supposed to be part of my life experience here, and the challenge is how I react to it.

I still remember the day when I soloed in my wheelchair. Abby, another therapist, had scrounged about and had come up with a wheelchair that fit me. With the length of my legs I needed one where my knees were not in my ears. Once outfitted with this new chair, I found I could move about much better.

With only one arm I first mastered wheeling around in circles, which came naturally. Sort of like the "blip" bird, afflicted with one wing shorter than the other, which causes the poor thing to fly in ever decreasing circles until it flies into it's own ass and goes "blip!" Only I could not get to the ever decreasing circles.

On my first solo I made it to pain and torture a bit late and too tired from getting there to do any work. I now had gained some more freedom and control over my life. That was, after all, why I was here. Everyone I met during those days had the same goals I did; Get me the hell out of here as soon as I am able. Although I'm pretty sure those helping me worded it as "Get him the hell out of here as soon as possible."

A hospital environment exacerbates your own private prison of fear about being there. The place has a rhythm much different from your body's. You find yourself trying to get a good night's sleep while some nurse is inserting an IV stint into the vein in your left arm. Again the teachings of the Gonzo Journalist Hunter S. Thompson helped. The drugs I ended up getting to help with the pain that was still hanging around would knock me out so I could get some sleep.

Living life in a hospital is both unreal and the most realistic it can get. You quickly accept your condition and take a weird solace that you are in good shape compared to some of those around you. You also want to help the newcomers. There are no fraternity initiation rites to get into this house. You survived them getting here. The survival process is really helped by a good sense of humor, however macabre it may be.

One day, I tried to leave my wheelchair several feet from my bed. I wanted it out of the way against the wall where it would not be in the way of those who wanted to visit. I was going to try to use my cane to get over to my bed. Getting up from the chair went okay. I was standing, at least. Then the floor started moving up and down, causing me to lose my balance and fall sideways into the wall. My left shoulder was against the wall. My right arm wasn't long enough to reach across my body and push me off the wall because I was leaning at too much of an angle. If I tried it, I'd fall to the floor. I was stuck.

"Hey, guys," I said to my roommates. "Call the nurse. I can't get off the wall."

"Look at how nice and stiff he is," offered DuPont.

"I would give this move a difficulty of four point three," mused Morin.

"He looks like a plastic Ken doll propped up against the wall," DuPont observed.

I was getting tired with the tightening of every muscle I could manage to keep from falling.

"Give me a break, you idiots," I pleaded. "I'm getting tired. I'm going to fall."

"Oh, the poor little grunt is tired and going to fall," said Morin. "We were much tougher in the Navy. We could stand like that for hours."

"Bet you a buck he doesn't fall for at least fifteen minutes," DuPont said.

"Listen, you shit heads. Call a nurse. I'm going to fall and break something."

"Nah, he'll go in another minute," said Morin, taking the bet.

They kept making book for at least a minute as

I became more scared and desperate. Eventually, I reasoned that if I was going to fall I might as well do it trying to get off the damn wall. I managed to roll so that I was at least facing the wall and could try a modified one arm push up off from it. Before I could do this, however, Angie barged in.

"All right," she said. "Who hit the button?" She hadn't noticed me yet.

The second she showed up we all became serious. Serious enough that I could push myself upright. Both Morin and DuPont had used their call button the minute they realized I was in trouble. The verbiage was just to give me gas while waiting for help to arrive. To turn off the call light Angie had to flip a switch by each of their beds.

"Okay, you two. What is going on?" She said, hands on hips, facing them with me behind her. Before either of them could say anything I chimed in.

"They were talking about your tits," I said.

"*What?*" she said, spinning to face me.

"Yeah. Morin said you had great tits and had the hots for DuPont."

Morin and DuPont were looking at me like I was an unreal person, their faces pale. They couldn't believe what I had said. *I* couldn't believe what I had said, but once you've started you have to finish.

"DuPont said you had shitty tits and didn't like him but liked Morin."

"*What?*" she said, spinning to face them again.

"Morin said they should call you in and that if DuPont talked dirty to you, your nipples would get hard."

"*What?!*" she said, her hands back on her hips.

"DuPont said you liked Morin the most and that *he* should talk dirty to you because you really like him the best," I concluded.

"I don't like either one of these assholes," Angie said, and stormed out of our room.

That afternoon, just before the day shift ended, DuPont got an enema and Morin got three shots that could have waited until the next day. I think Morin would have received an enema too if it wasn't for his colostomy. I think this type of activity is called male bonding.

If you have the right attitude, a hospital stay can be loads of fun.

I may be weird, or not as great a cook as I think I am, but I enjoyed the hospital food. Bernice, the hospital dietitian, did a great job. Her food system worked great. One day at lunch, DuPont complained about the little cup of peanut butter he always received during lunch. He liked peanut butter and had previously requested more after his special order peanut butter and jelly sandwich was found lacking. So every lunch he would receive the extra peanut butter, even if he was having soup. It came in a little plastic cup, one dollop from an ice cream scoop. He never sent the stuff back but would nibble on it throughout the day, though complaining with each bite that, "I wish they would stop sending me this fucking peanut butter." Every day he would ask the lad who delivered our meals to please stop sending him the peanut butter to no avail.

This particular day, lunch finished, Morin and I

were chatting, DuPont having wheeled himself out for a smoke, when Bernice came in.

"Bernice," I said. "Another great meal. Thanks."

"DuPont and I thought it was great too," said Morin. "Especially DuPont. He'd tell you himself but he's out smoking."

Where in the hell is he going with this? I thought. DuPont had spent his entire lunchtime bitching about the "fucking peanut butter".

"You know," continued Morin, "every day he teases us because he gets peanut butter and we don't."

Uh-oh. The plan of attack was getting clearer.

"I don't care for peanut butter myself," I said. "But DuPont is a nut for it, pardon the pun." My little contribution to the skirmish.

"Yep," said Morin. "The guy said just today he wished he could get more, not just with lunch but with every meal."

I thought he had gone too far and Bernice would know what we were up to. But she didn't. Most people complained about the food and the service and here were two guys who actually liked the food. Which we did.

"I think he has a screw loose, wanting peanut butter with every meal," I said.

"No way," said Morin. "When I was younger I used to have peanut butter with my eggs and catsup."

"You lie."

"No, it really tastes great," Morin said, sincerity dripping from every word.

"I'll see what I can do," said Bernice, after making notes

in the pad she always carried with her on her rounds.

At dinner that night DuPont had a cup of peanut butter to go with the corn beef and cabbage. That really set him off. Morin and I had to talk to him like Dutch Uncles to keep him in the room and not go down to the kitchen to complain.

The next morning when the lad delivering our breakfast lifted the cover on DuPont's plate he was greeted with a good sized plastic cup of the PB, arranged tastefully in the center of his scrambled eggs and slowly melting from their heat. The delivery boy was out the door to his food cart for the next plate before what he was seeing could register with DuPont.

"WHAT THE FUCK'S WITH THE FUCKING PEANUT BUTTER?" he screamed after the departing lad, who could offer no explanation upon his return with the next plate. DuPont had yet to notice the small cup of catsup for his eggs and peanut butter. Bernice did an excellent job of catering to the needs of her clients.

DuPont went berserk. He threw the cup of peanut butter out our door where it slid across the floor splattering warm peanut butter all over the place.

The veterans' hospital is a very clean environment, made so partly by the large floor cleaning and waxing machines that were forever prowling the corridors. At the moment that DuPont launched his cup of melted peanut butter out of the room, one of these prowling monsters was just passing through its trajectory.

The floor cleaning machine, which dragged its operator behind it and which wasn't designed for peanut butter, showed up just as the peanut butter cup came to a halt in its path. The machine seemed to like peanut butter much more than DuPont did. It tried to devour the small cup, but its digestive tract wasn't up to the job. So, like grass through a goose, it expelled the peanut butter and tiny pieces of the plastic cup in a swath as wide as the machine. To the machine, it was just another coat of wax.

The operator's shoes semi-bonded with the new coating of peanut butter and wax, with each step making a "smock" sound as they broke the suction of the peanut butter and wax coating. Hummmmmm went the machine. Smock, smock, smock went the operator, leaving foot prints in the coating. It took him eight to ten steps to figure out that something was wrong.

OSHA had ruled that to run one of these machines you had to wear huge earmuffs, so the operator couldn't hear the smock smock smock, he had to feel it. By then the area in front of the nurses' station was a mess. No-one seemed to know quite what to do for the first few seconds. The operator didn't turn off the machine, he just let go of it to head off on its own, leaving him standing stuck in peanut butter, looking down at his feet and trying to figure out why it was so difficult to lift them. The machine continued on its own until it ran into the wall. It would bump into the wall, backup for a couple of feet, and try again to make headway.

It took two different machines with two different operators the entire day to get the floor back to normal.

I was fortunate; most of the people with whom I

had contact really did care about their patients. One to whom I owe a great debt of gratitude, and my life, is Alfonse. His persistence and downright stubbornness in the face of my opposition probably saved my life for the second time in a few short months.

Alfonse took over Angie's place when her shift was over. The two were as different as day and night, which is an appropriate description. Angie female, Alfonse Male, Angie white, Alfonse black, Angie loud and excitable, Alfonse always calm and collected. While Angie could make a staff sergeant blush with her language, Alfonse was soft spoken and never swore. Alfonse was a good person to end the day with. Angie could give you coffee jitters without the coffee. Alfonse's demeanor would help you come down from the daily high you were on with all the activity directed at making you better.

The first thing Alfonse would do on entering our four bed asylum would be to empty our urinals. These were mass produced one-patient-use plastic things that were disposed of when you left. I thought this was just one of the crummy parts that came with the job. But he was checking our intake and output of liquids.

One day after checking my offering, he told me, "You are not peeing enough."

"If you want more pee, Alfonse," I said. "I'll drink more water."

"No, seriously," he said. "You're not voiding enough liquids"

"Don't try to confuse me with all your technical talk," I said. "I'm peeing as much as I can."

"We're going to have to check your bladder," he said,

leaving me wondering just what the hell the problem was. As far as I was concerned, everything was just fine in the peeing department.

Now there is ultrasound and there is ultrasound. Ultrasound as done by those who do it solely as a profession is not too bad. Ultrasound as done by someone who has very little experience and does so only on weekends can be grim. A professional will make sure the hard plastic wand is warm before applying it to your lower abdomen. Alfonse couldn't care less; he just wanted to see how you were doing bladder wise. A professional will use only as much of the slimy jelly used to make good contact with the wand as needed. To Alfonse, if a little was good, more was better.

I think he must have stored the little machine in the morgue. When he hit me with his magic wand it was cold enough to make me jump contracting all of my stomach muscles.

"Jesus, Alfonse," I said. "Where did you get that thing? It's freezing."

"It doesn't feel cold to me," he said.

"That's because you're holding the warm end."

The machine made all sorts of strange noises, a gurgling sound like some sort of mechanical indigestion. When it finished gagging, it would throw up a little paper diagram of my bladder with its estimate on the amount of pee stored within.

"When did you last void?" Alfonse asked.

"When did I what?"

"At what time did you pee into the urinal?"

"I don't know," I replied. "Sometime this morning?"

"Your chart says you voided three hundred cc's this morning. Now quit screwing around and tell me when you last took a piss." He was obviously tired of my smart ass attitude and wanted a straight answer.

"Alfonse, I don't know. Peeing isn't a black tie event with me, so I don't recall."

"From now on I want you to note when you void, so I can decide if you need a catheter."

Catheter! Now there is a word that will get most males' attention.

"Like hell," I said. "You're not sticking one of those things in me." I was trying to hide my fear.

"You don't have one small enough," offered Morin.

Alfonse ignored him. "I'll be fitting one if you don't void more," he told me.

Our dance of the pee or not to pee continued for a week. Then Dr. Brown came to see me.

"I want you to double void," he said.

"What the hell are you talking about?" I asked him. I had no idea what he was talking about. Double voiding was a new and exciting concept.

"Is that like in bridge when you don't think your opponent can make his bid, so you double?" I asked, trying to get into the swing of things.

"Yeah, something like that," he said. "I want you to wait a few minutes after you've voided and then try to go again."

"I can do that," I said. We were really making progress in the peeing department.

Everything settled down for a couple of weeks. I would attempt the vaunted double void, but no matter how hard I tried I could only seem to get the first half under control.

Since Alfonse wasn't bugging me, I hoped the whole thing had been dropped. Ah, but that was not the case.

One morning as I was snoozing before breakfast, Dr. Brown came in and asked me to roll onto my side and lower my pajama bottoms. I did so, and my reward for granting his request was a greasy finger inserted into my rectum.

"Good morning," came Dr. Brown's cheerful voice as he continued his prodding.

"Doc, I don't recall putting in a request for a rectal wake-up call," I said, somewhat distressed. "This is the rudest thing that's ever happened to me. Stop it."

"I want to check your prostate," he said.

"I would have preferred you started at the other end," I said. "Ouch. That doesn't feel too good." I was resigned to what was going on but, no matter how you experience this procedure, I can assure those who have not been the recipient of this gift, that it is entirely unpleasant.

"Yeah, it's a little enlarged," he said. "I think we had better get an ultrasound." He finally removed the offending digit.

Maybe there was nothing to worry about after all. My recently fondled prostate was only a little enlarged, and from the doctor's tone of voice it didn't seem to be a big deal. After all, I'd passed twenty some time ago and from what I had heard, an enlarged prostate was almost expected in older men.

There were, it seemed, many ultrasound labs, some

small, some large. The largest was in the wing where they did the X-ray. That was where the heavy duty stuff went on, and that was where I was wheeled around midmorning. I wasn't concerned as I had been here many times before with no dire consequences. I liked the technician. She had a great sense of humor and we joked a lot.

"How you doing this morning?" she said, as I was wheeled in.

"For my age and condition, fantastic," I said. It was my stock reply.

She wheeled me into the dimly lit examination room with all her computer screens, and held my wheelchair while I did the transfer to the table by myself.

"Good job," she said. "I see we are making progress. The last time you were here, you couldn't do that."

It was true. I now had the ability to go from wheelchair to bed, without assistance, without falling on my face. The floor no longer bounced as much as it did back when I ended up pinned to the wall.

We kept up some good-natured banter as she daubed a small amount of the gooey jelly on my lower abdomen and went to work. She covered a much broader area than Alfonse. Her machine, unlike Alfonse's, regurgitated little black and white pictures of what it saw instead of a line drawing.

She squirted some goop way up past my belly button.

"What the hell are you doing?" I said. "My prostrate isn't up there. It's a bit lower."

"I'm just looking around," was all she said, but I didn't like the way she said it. Something in the mood had changed. This wasn't an idle tour of my abdomen. A feeling of apprehension settled in the room. After a period of time, the machine spat out enough pictures to fill a photo album.

"What's up?" I asked.

"We got a problem here," she said, matter of factly.

"What's this 'we' shit, Kemosabe?" I said. "I'm the one on the table."

"Okay," she said. "You have an aneurysm, a big one, five centimeters. It's the size at which they operate."

I could think of nothing witty to say so I kept quiet.

"Don't worry," she said. "You're not going to die today or tomorrow. This thing has been in here for some time, so there's nothing to worry about."

I had spent thirty years in data processing as a systems engineer and as a consultant. I was used to taking information, either written or verbal, and breaking it down into its component parts. What I heard was *operate* and *no dying for a couple of days*. Or you only have a couple of days to live depending on whether the glass was half full or half empty. She did know how to get a persons attention. This dying and death stuff was a bit difficult to keep swallowing. I really wasn't ready to die so I concentrated on the good get well stuff. To have the possibility of death keep entering the equation was a trauma to my mental mood which usually managed to put a positive spin on my existence.

One result of my stroke was to provide me with a peaceful joy of life and in everyone around me. This was further heightened by the amount of medication

I was taking. But even with the mood altering drugs the on again off again death or no death was starting to wear me down. It was with mixed feelings that I returned to the ward and DuPont and Morin.

"How did it go?" they asked, or words to that effect.

"I have an aneurysm," I said, still unsure how long I had in this world.

"I had a friend who had one of those," said Morin.

"Oh, how is he?" I asked.

"Dead," was the reply. I didn't have long to live at all.

That afternoon, just after lunch, Dr. Brown showed up cheerful as ever and relaxed as always. He had a serene demeanor that only an eighth degree black belt in Karate should have.

Before I could open my mouth to ask questions, DuPont piped up.

"So, Doc," he said. "How long does he have. Can I have his boots?" which was really bizarre because DuPont had Multiple Sclerosis and not only couldn't walk but at times couldn't get his legs to bend.

"I got dibs on his jacket," said Morin, not wanting to be left out of the division of the booty.

"He's not leaving us yet, guys, so settle down," said Dr. Brown, pulling up a chair. Evidently we were going to have a chat.

"I hear we made some important discoveries this morning," the doc said as his opening gambit.

"Just what the hell is an aneurysm?" I asked. "I wouldn't know an aneurysm from an Alka-Seltzer."

"In your case, it's a swelling of the abdominal aorta. About five centimeters, I believe."

"Is it serious?" I asked.

"Yes and no," he said. "If it bursts it could be serious."

"Have you ever been involved with one that burst?"

"Three."

"And?"

"Two died and the third one would have been better off if he had," was the unsettling reply.

"I GET HIS BOOTS!" said DuPont, reasserting his claim.

"Shut up!" said Dr. Brown, and the comedy hour came to an abrupt end. I asked him how I would know if mine had sprung a leak.

"You'll get a lower back pain. Then you'll get cold. Then your lower extremities will go numb as your heart tries to supply your brain with blood but ends up pumping it into your gut. Then you'll pass out and die shortly thereafter."

Once again I had very little time left on this earth.

Dr. Brown had barely departed when another Asian man appeared, much more mature but equally handsome. I think the VA only hires good looking Asian male doctors, much to the delight of the female staff members.

"Hello," he said. "I'm Dr. Yoshi, vascular surgeon. I guess you're going to need a little attention."

He made it sound as if he was just another surgeon, one of thousands that populated these halls and was just stopping by because he was in the vicinity. In actuality, he was head of vascular surgery at the hospital. I liked him immediately, but then I liked almost every new person I met immediately, my rosy outlook being a gift from the large quantities of mood altering drugs I was constantly taking.

Dr. Yoshi explained that I really had no options and that surgery was required. Because of my recent stroke, however, he thought it better if we held off for a while. My opinion was different. After the recent uplifting talk I'd had with Dr. Brown about the three cases he'd been involved in, I wanted to get going as soon as possible. Any time within the next fifteen minutes was fine with me. But Dr. Yoshi held his ground. More tests were required before we could do anything. No matter how much he tried to reassure me that if I took my medicine and my blood pressure stayed down I was at minimal risk, I wasn't buying. I wanted *no* risk, minimal or otherwise. If I needed an operation to live, I didn't want to wait. I wanted it now. But he was the Big Kahuna, so the operation wasn't about to happen quickly.

What did happen was a constant parade of specialists by my bed, the most annoying of whom was the bright young lady assigned to use an ultrasound device hooked to a loudspeaker who kept trying to find a pulse in my left ankle with little success. The noise this device made when passing across a vein was not only annoying but very loud. It would really get to Morin, who was visibly slipping downhill.

Morin had just had half of his stomach removed and had more tubes and pipes in him than the Exxon Valdez. He kept trying to get someone to take out the largest tube which went into what was left of his digestive system. There was no doctor willing to mess with another doctor's work, even though the doctor who'd inserted the tube had left for an extended vacation immediately after doing so. This tube caused so much discomfort that it kept Morin awake the entire night and he was reduced to catnaps whenever he could get enough painkillers in him during the day. He was also getting an intravenous dosage of a blood thinner which made him violently ill. He was constantly vomiting bile.

All of this does not make a happy camper. The last thing he needed was to be jarred awake from one of his few naps by the sound of my blood coursing through a vein at 30 decibels over a loudspeaker. By the third or fourth such occurrence, he ventured an observation.

"I hope you fucking die soon so I can get some sleep," he said.

The specialist was somewhat startled by our humor.

As Morin became worse both DuPont and I became more vocal in his defense. Actually we were quite rude. It seemed that his doctor was back in town but had left instructions that he was not to be called except in an emergency. As Morin became grayer in color we spoke up more and more, attacking any doctor that entered the room in an attempt to get someone to do something.

DuPont finally got their attention by declaring to a visiting group, "I don't give a rat's ass how important you assholes think you are, I've contacted my attorney about your lack of attention to Morin. We're meeting tomorrow to sue all you miserable fucks out of your profession and respective houses."

That evening Morin's doctor showed up and promptly removed the offending tube with a quick yank.

DuPont wasn't the least bit polite to him. At one point asking the good doctor to come closer, "So I can kick the living shit out of you, you slimeball pig-fucking son of a bitch."

I think the doctor wanted a piece of DuPont also, but changed his mind when I chimed in, "And if he has any trouble, you sorry son of a bitch, I won't."

I outweighed him by a hundred pounds and he didn't know I only had one arm and one leg that worked. Consequently, our words hanging on him like a bad smell, he and his buddies left. By then Morin, minus the offending tube, had already started to get his color back.

The next morning we were paid a little visit by an administrative type who told us we were dangerously close to being kicked out of the hospital.

Morin, who was feeling much better now, started unhooking IV's and pulling tubes out of his nose.

"I'm out of here," he said matter of factly.

DuPont took a different approach. "What is your name again?" he asked. The administrative type told him, not yet realizing that threats that meant something to him and his self-importance meant jack shit to us.

"And what's your wife's name?" said DuPont, his tone far from impolite. Again, the administrative type told him, too late starting to realize that perhaps he shouldn't have bothered with this particular visit.

"Why do you ask?" he said, cautiously.

"I want to make sure we got both of your names right on the summons we serve you to sue your little tinkerbell ass off."

"You can't do that," Mr. Admin said, shaken.

"FUCK YOU," we all said in unison.

All in all, it was a fairly good day's work. And the day was just getting started.

I was heading out for my morning round of pain and torture when the second wave of attacking administrative types arrived. This one was pear-shaped, semi-bald, wore half frame glasses, and waddled instead of walking. Angie saw him before anyone else and planted herself in his path.

"Mr. So and So," she said. She didn't actually say so and so. She knew his name perfectly well. I just don't remember it. And don't care.

"How nice of you to visit," Angie said, in a voice that made me wary. Waddle-ass, too wrapped up in his own importance, didn't notice.

"We have a serious problem here," he said, "and it must be rectified at once." His tone was as ominous as a body shaped like that could make it.

"Oh, really? And what might that be?" It was difficult to believe these words were coming out of our Angie's mouth. They sounded way too polite.

"DuPont, Jackson and Morin have instigated a discharge offense," our new visitor said. "They are creating a disturbance, a very serious breach of hospital policy."

That was it. Our Angie returned from her polite vacation.

"Oh," she said. "Is that the policy where one of you administrative pukes tries to discharge patients without a doctor's concurrence? Or the policy where you hire incompetent doctors from outside because they're low bidders who care more about roasting hot dogs during the summer than they do for patients on whom they have operated, to the point where they must be threatened with a law suit just to get them off their sorry asses and in here to keep the patient from dying? Or is there some other asshole policy you've come up with that I don't know about?"

Angie was certainly up to speed regarding our little talk with the first administrative puke.

"I am putting you on report," he said with all the majesty he could muster.

"I don't care what you do, you lard ass son of a bitch," Angie said. "How dare you come on *my* floor and *my* ward and tell *me* what to do. Get your ass out of here before I kick it out. Go!" She took a threatening step toward him. He turned and beat a waddling retreat.

I started applauding, as did a couple of the nurses at the nurse's station who had been witness to the exchange. As old lard ass went by me I stopped clapping long enough to say as sweetly as I could, "Don't let the door swat you in the ass."

He was not agile enough and the door too swift. He got a good boost to help him along his way.

DuPont, who was having one of his leg-bending days, had hopped into his wheelchair and made it to the hallway just as Angie reached full stride in her delivery.

"Angie!" he shouted. "Marry me, you fiery bitch, and I'll make an honest woman out of you."

"Shut up, DuPont," she said. "You're already married."

"I'm not," I said, feeling I should put in a bid.

"Shut up, the both of you. You're both sick," said Angie.

"Oh good," said DuPont. "I'd hate to think I was in here under false pretenses."

"Be quiet, I have to check on Morin" she said

"I'm still here, darling. Will you marry me?" said Morin.

Not wanting to miss out on the excitement, he'd climbed out of bed and pushed his IV stand, loaded with little plastic bags and blinking machines to administer the stuff, to the doorway of our room where he joined DuPont.

"You're all sick," Angie repeated. "I need a cigarette. I'm going on break." And off she went, leaving her three suitors dejected.

It only took us a few seconds to get over our rejection, but it took us all a few minutes of silence to fully understand that our Angie had put her job on the line for us by telling the jerk who signed her paycheck to pound sand.

Without telling each other, we each, over the next couple of days, paid a visit to the Patient rep in a preemptive strike against universal assholedom on her behalf.

Nothing ever came of our little war. It died, as most wars should, without any casualties. Everything returned to what had become my new normal; Pain and torture in the morning, followed by futile attempts to get my arm to respond. It had sub-luxed permanently since my airplane flight. It had fallen out of the shoulder socket. Painful at times but for the most part it looked worse than it felt. The drugs I was taking masked any pain I might have.

DuPont started having trouble with his legs; they just didn't want to bend at the knees any more. Bracken remained the same, never saying a word as his stroke had affected his speech. He'd just look at his lunatic room mates with the usual blank expression.

At night after the captains and the kings had departed, we would be annoyed by Morin during TV time. Our room had two good sized TVs hanging from the ceiling, one for DuPont and I to enjoy and the other pointing at Morin and Bracken. We each had controls that allowed us to switch channels, alter the volume, and call our nurses. Once we'd all settled into our respective viewing patterns, Morin would start clicking through all the available channels. It was mildly annoying the first couple of times it happened, but both DuPont and I knew it was Morin rat-fucking us so we tried to ignore it. Bracken in the meantime would say nothing, just lie in bed with his blank look and watch the passing parade of channels.

Some nights though, the volume would be cranked up too and that *did* get to us. When the other TV hit the same channel DuPont and I were watching the room would fill with stereo sound, and then move on to noise with the next click of the remote. Bracken would just lay there while Morin would feign interest. This went on for over a week. Finally one night Morin rolled over and pretended to be asleep. The channels kept passing by on a regular basis.

"Morin, you sick son of a bitch," said DuPont, giving

in. "Quit fucking with the TV."

"It's not me," said Morin, gesturing towards Bracken. "It's that crazy fucker. Bracken, you crazy fuck, stop with the TV already."

Nothing. Bracken's stone face continued to stare at the screen. No matter how loud our protestations, nothing changed. We all hit our call buttons simultaneously, lighting up the alert board at the nurse's station like a Christmas tree. When this happens the nurses on duty really respond rapidly as it is usually a life or death situation. The night nurse was there in an instant, adrenaline pumping, ready for the emergency. What she got was three grown men tattling on another.

"Bracken won't stop fucking with the TV," we said. This was not what she expected. Old grown men crying over the TV. Bracken lay in his bed stone-faced, *click, click, click*. The nurse went over to Bracken's bed and asked him nicely, "Mr. Bracken, is there a particular show you would like to watch?"

Nothing changed, Bracken blankly staring at the television unblinking as various channels past in review.

"Mr. Bracken," she repeated a little louder. "Is there a particular channel you would like to watch?"

Nothing again. Just *click click click*.

"MR. BRACKEN" she fairly shouted" WHAT DO YOU WANT TO WATCH?"

Click click click.

"MR. BRACKEN, GIVE ME YOUR CONTROLLER!" she said, shouting in his ear, trying to take the controller away but Bracken had a death grip on the thing.

Without a word she left us alone with this madman TV junkie, returning minutes later with two very large male orderlies.

"Get that damn controller away from him," she ordered.

After a brief struggle, Bracken let go of his toy. Only then did his expression change. He blinked.

The next morning when the three of us returned from our pain and torture, Bracken's bed was empty, his name erased from the little sign outside our room giving the inmates' last names.

"What happened to Bracken?" Morin asked Angie.

"He was transferred to a nursing home," she said.

"Damn," said Morin. "I'm going to miss his happy smile and snappy chatter."

DOGS LOVE THERAPISTS

I was making progress, though still not as fast as I wanted. I could walk fairly well but needed to be able to walk further distances in order to get Beverly's blessing for discharge. So now the emphasis was on little walks during pain and torture. Besides, since my little aneurysm discovery I was constantly being reminded during therapy to stop holding my breath. That annoying habit would cause my blood pressure to skyrocket, which everybody but me knew was not what an aneurysm needed to stay in one piece.

I had been fitted with a brace for my left foot to keep the toes from dropping because, when they did, I would trip over myself. The toe drop symptom has me unexpectedly kissing the floor even today, but with the brace the incidence of tripping went way down and I graduated to stumbles. There is a significant difference between the two. With a trip, you're on your ass. With a stumble, you look uncoordinated but remain upright.

Beverly and I would spend our time together slowly traversing the many hallways of the complex. The hallway surfaces were asphalt tile, kept polished every day by those machines that went up and down the hallways dragging their operators behind them.

All the waiting areas to the many clinics were carpeted. There is where I could get in trouble. My shoes of choice were sneakers outfitted with elastic laces which allowed me to get them on after a protracted struggle. Walking was going faster than getting dressed. For some unknown but frustrating reason the mechanics of getting dressed was something I couldn't get down. It took me forever. I had emotional difficulty with someone helping me to get dressed, the part that bothered me the most being when a nurse knelt in front of me to put on my shoes and socks.

It took a long time to learn to traverse the carpeted waiting rooms. The rubber soles and toe of my sneakers were constantly getting caught in the carpet of the clinic waiting rooms. My brace didn't lift the toes up but kept the entire foot horizontal. It was up to me to get it up in the air. The problem comes in with the entire walking operation. It is really a mixed bag. Your right leg is operating automatically while the left is undergoing a learning experience which requires the damaged brain's constant vigilance.

My brain, still fighting for enough oxygen-rich blood to operate normally, would get tired and take a break, figuring that because the body had been walking fairly well for a number of years it could do so without constant monitoring. Unfortunately, the brain's little timeouts would usually happen was when I was on a roll. I'd be really moving along, doing well, and then suddenly the brain would take a mini-vacation and I'd take a spastic stumble, usually requiring Beverly's immediate intervention.

This would always happen in the carpeted waiting rooms filled with people. Whenever I recognized that a stumble was starting I would say, in my loudest theatrical voice, "STOP HITTING ME." Beverly would be very embarrassed, because the timing of the dance was such that people hearing my shout would turn just in time to see me awkwardly trying to catch my balance while this beautiful black woman was shoving me around. Or so they thought. She was really trying to grab hold of me to keep me from going down. Instead of *I'm falling*, Beverly's signal to grab me became *Stop hitting me*. She endured my antics for many days, but revenge would be hers.

Beverly decided that it was time for me to graduate from the level surfaces of the hospital to the unknown of the outside. I was concerned but couldn't delay the dreaded outside walk. No matter what my protestation, it would be met by Beverly's calm quiet refined voice firmly telling me that I could do it. It was another emotional hurdle I had to overcome, another fear to be faced and then conquered.

Beverly's voice was something else. She was very refined in her manner, never raising her voice as far as I knew, always the quiet voice gently encouraging you to work harder, to do one more repetition of your exercises.

The day came when I could no longer delay. Beverly pushed my wheelchair through the automatic door and there we were. Outside. It was one of those rare Seattle days; warm, the sun shining, big billowy clouds filling a very blue sky. The perfect day for our initial outing.

She locked my wheelchair and helped me stand up. She passed me my cane so I could maintain my balance and pulled the wheelchair back out of the way. She was just coming back to me when I suddenly got to see a side of Beverly I never knew existed.

Out of the parking lot bounded an extremely large dog. A Rotweiler. Now I am sure Rotweiler owners will sing the praises of the breed, but they possess a face that would give anyone pause. This thing was running at full tilt boogie covering a lot of ground quickly. A dog lover myself, I realized that this was the exuberance of getting free. The dog wasn't out to hurt anybody but just enjoying the feeling of running free.

Evidently Beverly was not a dog aficionado. The minute she caught sight of the animal, she exclaimed "I'm afraid of dogs. That dog looks mean," and opened the door quickly to re-enter the building. Realizing that the only danger was that if the beast came too close I could be knocked down and that Beverly, obviously afraid, looked silly peering out of the three or four inches of open door, I screamed, "DAMN IT, BEVERLY! DON'T LEAVE ME OUT HERE TO DIE!" which got me laughing. Beverly screamed back through the small opening, "SO LONG, SUCKA. YO LITTLE WHITE ASS BE DINNER!"

Now we both were really laughing. Beverly could talk street talk or whatever it was called with the best of them. We had a glorious time laughing and screaming at each other. Beverly also displayed a great sense of humor in describing at the top of her lungs just what part of my anatomy the dog would devour first. Plenty of people were witness to our fun, unprofessional though it might be.

When the dog left, Beverly emerged. While we were both trying to regain our composure, at which we weren't doing a great job, I attempted to step off a curb. I lost my balance and fell against Beverly. Actually, I fell *on* Beverly, my chin on top of her head and only her strength keeping me up. The laughter started again which robbed us both of the strength needed to get us out of the mess we were in. A man sitting on a close by bench asked if we needed any help.

"NO, I WANT TO FALL ON THIS BITCH AND SQUASH HER FLAT," I yelled, which sent us both back into hysterics.

Finally, Beverly regained her professional voice long enough to inform me that she would not be able to hold me up much longer. Now there was a very real possibility that I would squash her. So we both got serious and I got upright, standing on my own while Beverly retrieved my wheelchair. My first outside walk was a success. My Christmas card to Beverly was going to be a picture of a Rotweiler's face with the caption *feed me*.

One day, during a visit from Dr. Yoshi and an entourage of young female interns, I asked him to explain what my pending operation would consist of. I didn't like the sound of any of it. They would cut me open from stem to stern and rummage around until they found my aorta running from my heart somewhere underneath my guts to supply blood to the entire lower half of my body.

"This sounds like a serious pipe line," I said.

"It is," he said. "It supplies blood to your kidneys and to your legs. Your kidneys and your legs will be without blood for thirty minutes or so."

"Why?"

"We need to clamp off the aorta above and below the aneurysm, then cut it open, insert a tube made out of a GoreTex type of material, and then sew everything up nice and tight so you don't leak."

That was a little too much information for me to

comprehend. "What happens if I *do* leak?" I asked.

"We go back in and fix the leak," he said, as if it would be no big deal.

"Sort of like putting a patch on an inner tube?" I asked.

"Exactly. But don't worry, we do six to nine of these operations per month and no-one has leaked yet."

I felt better. "It sounds like a lot of us had better get serious about eating a healthy diet," I offered. "What are the risks?"

"Two percent die."

Wow, there it was again. I could die. But I'd tried that several months earlier and who was to say I would be any more successful at dying from this operation than I was from the stroke.

"Okay, what else?"

"Two percent can no longer ejaculate," he calmly replied.

He had my undivided attention. Now we were getting into the really serious male quality of life style stuff.

"You mean I wont be able to get a hard on?" I said, ready to die rather than face this little procedure.

The female doctors in his entourage tried not to blanch at my question. The VA was a teaching hospital for the University of Washington medical school so many of the doctors we met were just getting started in this honorable and lucrative profession. Dealing with aging veterans moves them toward their goal very rapidly. Dr. Yoshi was always accompanied by an entourage of these young things. So young, so fresh, so semi-pure. I don't think the purity part lasted long at all. It was up to people like me to assist in the maturation process.

"No," Yoshi said. "You would be able to achieve an erection but you would not be able to ejaculate."

"Would there be any feeling?" I asked, wanting to know all there was to know.

"Yes. You would still have the feeling of the climax, you just wouldn't ejaculate."

I was able to stop holding my breath. "Sort of like a seriously complicated vasectomy?" I said.

"Exactly."

"Hell," I said. "Then there's nothing to worry about. I'll just fake it. Women have been doing that for centuries. Isn't that true, doctors?" I looked innocently at the now uncomfortable interns while Dr. Yoshi enjoyed a sly little smirk.

Dr. Yoshi went on to tell me that the time I was here getting stronger would be well spent for there would be many a test I'd need to have before they could open me up. Oh swell, I thought, the fear of the unknown test taking center stage in my mind.

I related this conversation to both Morin and DuPont, both of whom had advice for me.

"Don't ever let them put you on the third floor," Morin said. "The people who work there are not human. They don't have normal parents, they never made it out of high school, they glow in the dark. They're dropouts from an unaccredited veterinary college. I had to spend three months there and I never want to go back." He actually sounded scared when talking about the third floor which made what he said sound even more ominous.

"Don't let them give you the bleeding test," offered DuPont. "I had a buddy they gave it to and he almost died. In your condition, you just might."

"What the hell is a bleeding test?" I asked, focusing on that rather than Morin's warning about the subhuman species populating the third floor.

"I really don't know but they cut you and see how long you can bleed before you pass out," DuPont said with complete assurance that he had correctly described a procedure about which he knew absolutely nothing.

These two were a never ending source of valuable information, but my stay with them was about to come to an abrupt end. I had been suffering from diarrhea for several days and, as my two amateur guidance counselors were about to offer more insights, they were interrupted by Angie barging into the room.

"Hey, bug man," she said. She was addressing me.

"What do you mean?" I asked.

"You have parasites."

"I know," I said. "They're right here." I gestured at Morin and DuPont.

"No, you asshole," she said. "You're full of bugs eating you up."

"Oh, swell. Now what?" I didn't know if this was serious or not. Angie seemed too pleased with the information for it to be false.

"We are going to quarantine your ass," she said with glee.

Within moments I was secured in my own private room with my own TV and toilet. Hell, I thought, Parasites aren't all that bad.

They weren't. But the antibugotic I was forced to take was the foulest tasting stuff I had ever put in my mouth. The taste stayed with you long after you swallowed the pills. The pills had a systemic quality that soon had you smelling like the foul taste. About four days into my ten day treatment I begged Dr. Brown to change the prescription. But the staff parasitologist said that this was the only thing that would cleanse my system of these voracious little friends that could multiply faster than rabbits.

Angie took pleasure in coming into my room first thing in the morning to give me direction.

"Okay, Jackson. Time to shit in the hat."

The hat was a plastic gasket that fit under the toilet seat and over the bowl with a depression that when turned upside down did indeed make it look like a plastic hat, a white replica of those worn by Korean farmers. I was always afraid that my volume would be greater than the device's capacity. But some real engineering had gone into its development and this never happened.

Hospital life became dull after my move. I no longer had Morin and DuPont to interpret the day's events for me, broadening my horizons with alternative viewpoints on just about everything. Now my schedule was my own, except for the evening pill nurse. The Hospital had a schedule for dispensing medications and I was damn well going to follow it even though I would often fall asleep hours before the schedule said I was ready for my medications. The meds included my sleeping pill, which I really needed to stay asleep through the left leg spasms that were still with me. The pill nurse was a real pain in the ass and I don't care if I never see her face again. I hope she wasn't as inflexible at home with her husband and kids but, as far as I was concerned, she would have fit right in at Buchenwald.

There were other jerks populating the hospital staff but God must have thought I'd suffered enough and mercifully let me stay out of the way of most of them.

My son would visit me quite often, most of the time bringing my little grandson with him. This grandchildren stuff was a new experience for me but I was happy with my reaction. I didn't think it could be possible to love someone else's child as you had your own. I took pride in the nurses fussing over him. Angie wouldn't let go of him, she carried him around introducing him to everyone. I wonder if that experience will scar him for life. Angie gave the lad his first lecture on sexually transmitted diseases when introducing him to Morin and DuPont. The short but graphic lecture probably could have waited for several more months. I am sure there would have been better comprehension on his part.

I don't know why but I was constantly surprised when I found someone else who had experienced a stroke, perhaps because there seemed to be so many of us. During one of my sons visits, back when I was rooming with Morin and DuPont, the four of us were discussing the various physical effects of a stroke,

"When I had my stroke," Morin said, "the only thing I could say was 'spoon'."

"It's a shame you got better," offered DuPont.

"I wish that was all my dad could say," said my son. Truly his father's son.

"Traitor!" I said with as much reproach as I could muster under the circumstances.

It was true I had become a regular Chatty Cathy. My ex-wife used to say "So many men and so little time" as a joke, now no longer funny. In that same vein, now for me at least, there was so much to experience and talk about and so little time. Even if I live another fifty years I don't think this quiet desperation will ever leave me. I don't want it to. Just being here is a more intense high than it ever was. Since my stroke I have no time for garbage. It's as if a sort of emotional spring cleaning has taken place. I have neither the time nor the inclination to have junk in my life. Even this takes practice. Some of this junk includes people and I am still learning how to move them out of my life with as little damage to them as possible. Worried that I was nuts, I spent some time talking this over with Morin, my more sensitive room mate.

His advice was succinct. "Fuck 'em," he said. But he went on to elaborate. "I had a friend. We were in the Navy together, I was in his wedding, he in mine. But over the years we changed. I grew to dislike him, but I kept living in the past, the good old days. It was only our past that sustained our present. After my stroke I was like you are; just happy to be here. Then one day, after my long time friend had fucked me over for the last time, I told him to get the hell out of my life. He couldn't understand what had happened because over the years I'd always allowed him to screw me over as

I held on to our history instead of acknowledging our present. It turned out to be the best gift I ever gave myself. He was an asshole and I finally acknowledged the fact. We would have never become friends if we were to meet in the present. I have a much cleaner, happier life without him in it. Like you, I worried about the other person's feelings, and could have gone about the separation in a more hospitable manner, but we can learn how to do that also."

"Jesus, Morin," I said, somewhat in awe at this insightful look into his psyche. "That was certainly a mouthful. Hit a hot button, did we?"

"Fucking A. Get rid of the jerks and assholes that are buzzing around you. They're feeding off you to keep alive. Take away their food and they die."

"Morin, you existential prophet," I said. "I didn't know you were capable of such deep thought."

"Existentialism has nothing to do with it. Start listening to your gut; sometimes it's smarter than your brain."

If you're lucky, a hospital stay can be a learning experience but, learning experience or not, my stay would be coming to an end soon. I had made good progress learning to walk, even though I unfortunately needed a cane to do so. My gut was telling me that if I could walk across a room I could walk any where. Thankfully my brain overrode that inclination. Little or no progress was being made with my arm and I was learning how to live without it. Not a good sign, I reasoned. If I could operate somewhat successfully with just one wing there would be a good chance that I would accept that way of life rather than keep the goal of two arms working in front of me.

Also, hospital life no longer had any fascination for me. It had become routine. Even the new tests were now accepted as routine. My soul was getting my body ready for the outside world.

There were, however, new and wonderful events that would keep me a boarder here a bit longer. I got a rash all over my body. Thankfully it didn't itch much. It just felt like I had individual pieces of sand stuck to me. My skin was no longer smooth, more like sandpaper. Dr. Brown was notified. His visit was like most. He arrived happy and upbeat, and departed somewhat perplexed. I think it was because he took every thing I said seriously.

"Hmm," he said. "How did you get this?"

"Angie gave it to me. She said there was no need for a condom."

"Well," he said, with a pause to digest this unsettling news. "I don't think it is sexually transmitted."

"Thank God," I said. "We were planning on getting married. We want to have children, Angie loves children. This thing wouldn't make them brain damaged or anything, would it?"

I was way over the bounds of accepted behavior here and Dr. Brown, used to dealing with normal sick people, was out of his element. He'd seen enough and heard too much. He left and, within seconds, Angie barged into my little room.

"Jackson, you son of a bitch," she said. "What did you say to Brown? He asked me if I had a rash too."

"YOU BETTER LEAVE THE DOOR OPEN,

DARLING. PEOPLE ARE STARTING TO TALK," I responded, loud enough so everyone at the nurses station could hear.

"You miserable bastard. I'd have been better off if you died."

"Have I ever told you your eyes sparkle when you're excited?"

I didn't know you could slam a heavy hospital room door that hard. I don't think she'd found it a joyous encounter. It was several days before she returned to me.

One day when it was her turn in the barrel, Abby in physical therapy observed, "It appears that you are getting ready to go home."

"What do you mean?"

"You're complaining more about what's going on."

"I am?"

"Yep. It's a sure sign that you've made all the progress you can on this stay."

I really liked Abby. I liked all the other new people who were helping me too, but I liked Abby more. I wanted to know more about her as a person, not just as a therapist who was helping me learn how to walk. I am sure that there was a part of my infatuation that was normal. Like a woman falling in love with her gynecologist, or a man falling in love with the female shrink to whom he has gone to help him relate better to women. During all my awkward attempts to get to know her better, Abby was unfailingly polite. Putting up with this type of garbage had to be hidden somewhere in her job description.

Making no progress with her, the half of my brain

that was working right started trying to convince everyone that I needed continuing help, especially when I returned to Costa Rica, and that the VA should provide me with my own personal therapist. This request didn't fly. It did not even get to taxi to the runway.

Abby herself would just smirk when I tried the direct approach. "You should come with me to Costa Rica," I'd say. "It's warm there, and my house is very remote. You could get an all over tan."

I gave her coffee to see if that would help break the ice, but it got me nowhere, except perhaps in keeping her from filing a grievance about what was arguably harassment, no matter how heartfelt and sincere it may have been.

I would never find out what her favorite food was, or if she enjoyed classical music. Or, even more daring, if she was a grouch first thing in the morning. For all I knew she was living with someone. That I didn't want to know, so I never asked. The answer could have broken my heart.

Ah, puppy love.

Somewhere at some time, someone had added "drive a car" to my to-do list. Good thinking. How else would I get to my house in southern Oregon? It took me some time to find the driving office. As usual, without the advice of DuPont and Morin to guide me, I was flying blind. So I wheeled myself back to my old asylum for the benefit of their instruction and guidance.

"Watch out for the driving instructor," Morin warned me. "She's a seventy year old, three hundred pound nymphomaniac who'll drive you out into the woods and kick your ass if you don't agree to be her kinky sex slave. She loves oral sex, or so I'm told."

I had definitely been in the hospital too long, as this didn't sound all that threatening.

DuPont's advice was even more gross. I'll spare you.

So, armed with this valuable knowledge, I set out to find the office of this sex goddess. It's odd that it proved to be so difficult because it turned out I passed by the place every day on the way to pain and torture. Finally, once it dawned on me that the sign that said Driving Lab was probably where I wanted to go, I tried to get inside. The door was locked tight. Someone must have warned her I was coming. But my persistence paid off and we eventually made connection.

Upon our first meeting, I saw that she was neither seventy years old nor three hundred pounds, though I did hope that there might be some truth to the nymphomaniac part. She was good looking, with what I would call a Spartan figure, nothing in excess.

On this first visit I learned that it was her job to re-certify my driver's license. If I didn't pass all the tests she would notify the department of motor vehicles to revoke my license. That got my attention. I would willingly take drivers education again. First I had to prove that my reaction time was within normal bounds. I had to prove that I had made progress from those first days after the stroke when cognition came slowly.

To do this, I was squeezed into a driving machine consisting of a seat, a steering wheel, a gas pedal, clutch and brake. Again, because of my length, I did not quite fit. It was quickly determined that my driving my beloved import truck was a thing of the past. There was no way on God's green earth I would be able to depress a clutch with my left leg operating as it did. In addition, my size fourteen feet were too big; I would hit the brake pedal when depressing the accelerator. I had to bend my right foot at an unnatural position to keep from operating both pedals simultaneously. But once I mastered this we were ready for the test.

There were two lights where the dashboard would be in real life, one red, the other green. I would depress the accelerator until the green light would come on, then slam on the brake when the red light came on. The machine would print out my reaction time after each try. The time to beat was seven-tenths of a second. I came in at five-tenths or less on my attempts. I had graduated to a real live driving test on the streets of Seattle. We would do that the following week. I would not have passed this test if I'd had to operate the accelerator with my right foot and move the clutch with my left. I was now limited to automatic transmissions.

When I wasn't singing for my living, one of the best jobs I ever had while in college was driving a set of doubles during the summer months for Western Milk Transport. This rig consisted of the tractor and a couple of three-thousand gallon milk tanks following. I drove a school bus during the school year and, during summer vacation, drove a tractor and two tanks of milk from Santa Barbara (where I was going to college) to the creamery in Los Angeles. It was almost sixty-five feet long and weighed in at just under sixty-five thousand pounds.

Although there'd be no more sixteen gears forward for me, I'd taken pride that I could handle the big rig and go through the sixteen gears without leaving any metal on the pavement, so I was pretty sure I could handle an automatic, even using just one arm. Saying it is a lot easier than doing it. If you are not used to the automobile, it has a tendency to be in a different spot than it was when you took your hand off the wheel for a brief second to turn on the turn signals. I found this out before we were out of the hospital parking lot.

On the day of my driving test I didn't know if I could get my wheelchair into the trunk. I had never tried before but I figured I could lift it and somehow throw it in. As luck would have it my instructress did not have the keys for the trunk and there was no inside latch as far as I could tell. I sat behind the wheel as my instructress pushed my wheelchair back inside. Again my old friend stupid showed up. This was a brand new car with all the bells and whistles and I had only until my instructress returned to try to figure out what all the levers and knobs were about. Actually this turned out to be just what I needed to knock the cocky shit out of my system. When she got in the car I said, "Look, I'm trying to get over a stroke so I don't know if I'm doing alright or not. Please let me know. A stroke can make you a little goofy, you know. It scrambles your brain."

"That's the right attitude," she replied. "You'd be surprised how many of the older men I have to flunk because they think that they have been driving for years and know more than I do about driving. Especially the CVAs; many haven't realized that their brain was damaged, not just an arm or a leg. They are a danger to themselves and everyone on the road when they're behind a wheel. If you just take it slowly and don't do anything too quickly, you should be okay."

Thank you, God. It was a very sedate drive, and one which I passed, though in retrospect I scared the living daylights out of my self.

Now occupational therapy wanted to make sure I could fend for myself in the real world. I would have to prove that I could get on and off the toilet and into and out of the shower. I would also have to prove I could cook without catching the kitchen or myself on fire.

Before my stroke I took pleasure in my cooking ability. Cooking with just one wing, however, kind of throws a monkey wrench into the whole equation. Try chopping an onion using only one hand. The damn things know how to escape. At the first feel of the knife they scamper off the chopping block. In addition you have one arm just hanging there which at the very least throws off your aim and the arm can, for some unknown reason, always end up in the middle of things when it's not needed. For my first test I was asked to make biscuits from a biscuit mix. There was cinnamon and sugar in the lab's kitchen so I made cinnamon rolls instead. For my next trick, I fried an egg. So far, so good. I could live on cinnamon rolls and fried eggs. Much later, when really on my own, I found that the reality is that, when left to your own devices, you cook any frozen dinner that you can throw in the microwave without it catching fire. Why didn't we just practice microwave?

Next, I had to show that I could get my wheelchair

into and out of a car trunk. First I was asked to lay it on top of one of the workout tables. There was no car in the occupational therapy lab. For once my length worked in my favor. I found that, if I placed the collapsed chair at my right side up against my leg, I could reach across through the opposite wheel and grab hold of the seat brace. Standing upright would lift the chair several inches off the floor and then all that was required was to brace the chair against my hip and lift to get it horizontal. From this position it was easy to slide it on to the table. Moving day was approaching.

I had been given a target date for my discharge, still several weeks off. I would be leaving a safe haven, no matter how unreal, for the unknown once again. Only this time there would be no one waiting to help me if I got into trouble. And somehow I knew I would manage to get into trouble. The thought of being on my own still scared me. My future goal had to be to not put myself in a position where I could kill myself. That eliminated rewiring my house.

Before I could leave, there was something else I had to submit to. All the tests requested by the many doctors had to be completed before I could leave, and this included the dreaded bleeding test and having my blood lit up so they could get a good picture of my aneurysm. Both tests sounded worse than they were. Only now there was no Morin to provide invaluable guidance. The bastard had gone and gotten himself well, so they'd kicked him out.

DuPont, on the other hand, wasn't feeling too good. He was itching to go home but the powers that be wouldn't let him. One day, on arriving early to pain and torture, I found him just lying on the workout table doing nothing.

"Come on DuPont," Abby was saying. "Get moving."

Nothing, he just lay there. While I could walk with a cane, it still was dangerous and I had very little energy to remain upright for any length of time. I spent most of my time in my wheelchair. So I wheeled myself over and asked him, as discreetly as I could, "Hey, buddy. What's up? Why aren't you doing your exercises?"

I knew that if he didn't do the exercises or at least attempt them that pain and torture would not sign off on his discharge. He knew it too but no longer cared. We talked for a while and I got him to make a half hearted attempt to do some exercises. But as I left, I turned to see him just lying there again. After that experience I was very sad.

The bleeding test took place in a basement lab on the same level as the morgue, which was more than enough to unnerve me. The technician who administered the test was pleasant and polite. She explained that indeed I would be cut, but the goal was to measure how long it took my blood to coagulate. This explanation did nothing to alleviate my fears.

"Don't worry," she said. "It's a tiny cut and you'll hardly feel it."

I had heard that too much in the past. Like when the doctor says, "You might feel a little discomfort." I wonder what Madison Avenue guy thought that little phrase up. It really means "This shit is going to hurt like hell."

She pulled out a little plastic box and pressed it against the inside of my right forearm. There was a snap. I jumped, and started bleeding from two tiny cuts. The goal was to stop bleeding within ten minutes. No sweat, I thought. That was before I started taking blood thinners. I stopped bleeding just at ten minutes. I had passed the test. Now on to the next one, and then freedom.

Lighting up my blood. I had no idea what that entailed. I found out soon enough that it included inserting an intravenous needle into my left forearm. Better my left than my right. At least my left arm was good for that. This happened just before midnight the evening before the test. I was awakened by a little lady sticking me with the needle. I was taking enough painkillers in order to stop my leg convulsions that I hardly felt it. I went back to sleep, her apology for waking me drifting off as I did so.

The next morning I was wheeled down to X-ray were I would be shoved into a "bat can" machine. A slight problem cropped up when we realized I could not move my left arm out of the way to fit into the metal donut's hole. There was some swearing involved when they had to bend me into a very unnatural position before enough of me could be inserted for the pictures. My blood was to be joined by some radioactive gas which would make the aneurysm stand out when bombarded by Bat Can rays.

The device containing the radioactive gas could only have come from a nineteen thirties Flash Gordon movie. It consisted of transparent cooling fins surrounding an eight inch long tube that came to a point where a coil of plastic tubing was attached. The plastic tube had a large needle at the business end that was pushed into the IV in my left arm. I didn't have to go back for a second stuffing, so I must have passed that test too, even though getting out of the machine proved as difficult as getting in. The main reason being that my body was incapable of assisting. Those muscles needed to do so had not reawakened yet.

During those last few days, Angie remained Angie, still giving me shit. However a slight overtone of gentleness had managed to creep into her voice and mannerisms. On the afternoon of my departure, I went hunting for her. I wanted to thank her for being the consummate professional as well as a good friend. She was still on duty, but nowhere to be found. She must have been hiding, perhaps afraid to give me one last shot at her. The world needs more Angies in it.

I wheeled myself into the old room to say good bye to DuPont. He was non-communicative, preferring to just lay there. I don't think he even bothered with Pain and Torture any more. His new roommates were singularly unimpressive, sullen in their own way. There was no longer joy in the room and I left as quickly as my conscience would allow. That last visit was very uncomfortable. There was a resigned sadness that stayed with me for too long. I wanted my goodbyes to encompass the joy and excitement I felt at my graduation to the real world. That desire proved to be unrealistic as those I said goodbye to would remain in their present unreal world not feeling the joy of leaving within themselves until it actually arrived.

My goodbyes to Beverly and Abby were like sweet and sour soup, the opposing tastes commingling in each spoonful. They seemed to feel some of my joy, maybe because they had been the most effective in their treatment and could see my progress.

As usual, I felt tongue tied trying to tell Abby thank you and goodbye. So I called her Pokey, referring to Pocatello, Idaho, where she'd received her post-grad education in what she now did so well. I offered her one last chance to come to Costa Rica and endure all sorts of depravity. She again deferred with the grace of a lady.

With Beverly, I just gave her a hug and barked softly in her ear. She got the message.

I knew during all the goodbyes that all of these people were special. They were driven by a most noble desire to help their fellow man. To do so they were willing to endure miserable working conditions with more bureaucratic bullshit than any human being should be forced to endure in a lifetime. They did it with grace, compassion and love and I will never forget any of them. When God stops teasing me with death and the inevitable arrives, I will still be forever grateful for the gift they have given me; the second half of my life. Or, more correctly, a second life. It will be much different from the first but, like the first, will be full of learning, overcoming challenges, excitement and wonder at the joy of just being here.

My son again took off from work early to retrieve me. He wheeled me to the car where we met with a little difficulty getting my wheelchair into the back seat. After some struggle and appropriate swearing the thing slid in. I was as a child. The excitement and overwhelming joy was fantastic. It had no bounds, completely engulfing my soul, an orgasm of feeling that I struggled to control so that I wouldn't be recommitted for a mental evaluation. I would have to return soon enough as the aneurysm time bomb ticking within me was still there.

We drove directly to the car rental agency. I was sure they would refuse to rent me a car even though I had been officially certified as a safe driver by the Veterans Administration. I had to wear a large plastic claw like device on my left hand to keep it from balling up into a painful fist.

I was scared that when I hobbled in to rent the car, providing I made it up the two steps into the office, the clerk would refuse to rent me a car. I had yet to learn about a piece of enlightened legislation called "The Americans with Disabilities Act." I hadn't yet accepted that I was disabled.

In fact, renting the car proved to be a no-brainer. There was only an ever so brief moment when I feared the clerk would say no. To appear normal, I used my right hand to lift my left arm onto the counter, plastic claw and all. Unfortunately this was the time that my left arm decided it was its turn to throw a spasm. It swept out away from my body, across the counter, clearing it of maps, writing tablets, and applications for credit cards.

"I sent it to obedience school but it was just a waste of money," I said, hoping to defuse the situation as my son hurriedly cleaned up the mess.

I was given the keys to a brand new car, again with

more bells and whistles than I could comprehend. My son leaned in the open door and quickly explained what I was looking at. With that we were off.

Talk about culture shock. It was the evening rush hour. It took all the concentration I could muster just to follow my son's car as we picked our way through the packed Seattle streets. There was a good possibility that I would have become separated from my son had it not been for the courtesy of the Seattle drivers, even though there were the occasional jerks, recent transplants to the Pacific Northwest.

If the surface streets in Seattle were bad, the West Seattle freeway was hell on wheels. No one seemed to pay attention to the speed limit. The speed scared me. I had to remind myself that I had done this before and that there was a good chance I wasn't going to die in the next minute or so. "My God," I thought. "If this is a Thursday night I wonder what a Friday night is like, when these people are not just rushing home but rushing toward a weekend."

I arrived at my son's house thoroughly shaken, parking in the alleyway up behind his house for the downhill trip into the house, my daughter in law and grandson there to greet me. I don't think the little lad really knew or cared who I was, but I felt loving towards him when I saw his happy little face. I was truly blessed to have this woman and child in my life. No matter how brief. I am a very lucky man.

We spent the evening watching television and eating pizza. My son loaded the car with the plastic crates brought back from Costa Rica. Then we went to bed. I had trouble getting to sleep, the excitement of the next day's journey keeping me awake, but my tired body and the strong medicine provided by my dear friends at the VA helped. My body had enough for one day and gave out on me, so off to sleep I went.

 I wanted to get an early start for the seven hour drive to Grants Pass, Oregon, where I live when in the states. I got up with my son who was at work every morning by seven AM. We talked briefly, enjoying a cup of coffee together, both of us with our private thoughts and the understanding that this could be the last time we would enjoy each other's company.

 Since my stroke, we both have come to the realization that our existence here could end at any moment. This new mindset heightens normal activity so it becomes more intense and meaningful. The act of enjoying a cup of morning coffee with your son fills you with so much emotion that the memory of the moment can be enjoyed long after the event has passed. When he left for work, I left for my home in the States.

 It took me until Olympia, an hour south of Seattle, before I realized that driving was no longer an automatic function. I couldn't turn my head to admire something whipping by because my hands would follow my head. This was particularly hazardous when passing a truck on it's left. Out of habit, I would look through the passenger side window to check their tires. In doing so, I would move closer to the truck tires. They would grow increasingly larger in the right side passenger window until only the metal wheel was visible. The rubber part of the tire would be above the top of my car before it would dawn on me that perhaps I needn't be this close. Thankfully I was on the road before the rush hour as I needed the space for my constant lane hopping. The worst and most dangerous part of the drive was when I moved into the lane on my left. For some reason I never readjusted the mirror, so there was a blind spot. I think I only had three drivers honk at me for abruptly showing up inches from their front bumper but that was three too many.

By the time I reached the Columbia River, the border between Washington and Oregon, I was into the swing of things. The car was equipped with cruise control which allowed me to change my sitting position, thereby avoiding painful cramps in my legs, something I'd always had to endure on long road trips because of the length of my legs.

Passing through the Portland suburbs, I stayed on interstate five heading south to Salem, Albany and Eugene. It was a vibrant early June day, the new green colors of spring everywhere and the sun warming my new world, my new approach to life. The billowy clouds provided shade for a brief respite from the growing warmth of the day. Nostalgia was my companion as I thought about my recent journey through two hospitals and the people I had met along the way, though I allowed myself to feel a little anxiety about my forthcoming triple-A operation.

I thought about all the crazy things that Morin, DuPont and I had inflicted on those around us. Why would grown men be so silly? It was then I realized why I had been so nuts, and figured that my roommates must have had the same response. I was afraid of where I was in my life's journey, afraid that I would not lead a normal life again, afraid to accept death as being ever so close. Afraid I would no longer have my enjoyment of life. Afraid of growing old and unable to take care of myself, a burden on my family, afraid to face the reality that I was no longer the person I had been. Afraid of dying an invalid or a slow lingering death, afraid that I would never escape from the prison of growing fear into which I had been thrown by my stroke and, last but not least, afraid of the unknown. Fear could be distracted by our goofy pranks, held at bay with our laughter. Getting out of the hospital was a signal that there might still be opportunities ahead, more laughter not to hide fear but to express joy.

Passing through Eugene and on into the foothills of the Siskeyou Mountains some five hours into my journey of reflection and dissection, I realized I was no longer held prisoner by my stroke. I was free to live again, to learn and, possibly, to love again. I had, since the end of my marriage, learned to live alone. I loved the solitude but realized that I am not a solitary person. I now understood just how much I missed sharing. As I would see a particular scene, I wanted to point it out, to discuss how it was affecting me and see if the feeling was experienced by another. There was no one beside me to share the moment with. I enjoyed thinking about the possibility that perhaps I would find someone again to share with. What a seductive feeling to be filled with, sensual in its connotations. As I climbed into the mountains into the magnificent stands of evergreens I started singing an old Mamas and Papas tune from the sixties, "Go where you want to go, and then do what you want to do..."

I was free from the dungeon in which my stroke had thrown me. Fear, my companion of so many months, had grown tired of me, left without saying goodbye. As I sang I recalled the television clip of the greatest speech I had ever heard, Dr. Martin Luther King Jr. in Washington, DC:

"Free at last, Free at last. Great God almighty, Free at last."

By the time I reached my home in Grants Pass, Oregon that evening, I was exhausted. The drive had taken just over eight hours. I had not had to concentrate this long since before my stroke. Eight hours of trying to stay alert had taken its toll on my still slow-working brain. I took the medicine I needed to take in the evening, took off my clothes, climbed into bed and was asleep instantly.

The next morning started early. After so many months in strange beds, my own bed seemed strange and sleep the first night was fitful. When I swung my legs onto the floor next to my bed my body followed and I ended up kissing the rug. As I lay in the carpet somewhat confused I slowly made plans for getting myself upright. While the fall was not expected the situation was not one that elicited any panic on my part. After several minutes of struggle I managed to get myself back into bed. Except for the normal struggle of getting dressed the rest of the morning went quite well. I stumbled a few times while walking around the house but did not fall.

At noon, my neighbor Jackie and I drove down to the Medford airport to return my rental car.

Jackie was a beautiful young thirty-something divorcee from Britain with an engaging accent, short blond hair, and a fantastic body that featured breasts that were much too large for her five foot three frame. We had become good friends as neighbors. Whenever one of us would go to the store, we would ask the other if there was anything we could get them. Jackie would occasionally confide in me her latest romantic escapade with her boy friend. This always made me envious of the guy.

On our return trip from the airport I was forced to explain in detail why I needed a cane to walk. Jackie was a registered nurse who worked in a Medford hospital. When she heard the details of my stroke, she became very concerned and promised to take care of me. She demanded a key to my house, so I gave her a spare key when we returned. The short drive left me exhausted so I took a nap when Jackie returned to work.

That evening I found a bottle of martinis in the door of the refrigerator and to celebrate my return to freedom I had a couple or three. When I got up out of my chair after the last one, I passed out and fell face down on the floor. When I came to, my nose was bleeding, staining the rug. I was unable to get up but I managed to reach the cordless phone on the table besides my chair and called 911.

I did not realize that when a 911 ambulance arrives at your door they don't turn off the flashing lights that light up the neighborhood. This was not the type of attention I enjoy, but the lights did bring Jackie and the key to the front door so a forced entry was not necessary. The two professional medics that had arrived to save my life had a hard time doing their job due to the beautiful distraction of Jackie in a cotton T-shirt and no bra.

Although I had learned to appreciate the well developed bottom while in Costa Rica, as a teen I had developed a permanent fondness for the top part of a woman's anatomy. I was used to seeing Jackie braless beneath almost transparent shirts. Every evening upon arriving home from work, Jackie would take off her bra and cover herself in something comfortable. As she explained, the bra straps cut into her shoulders and caused her considerable pain; thus no bra at home. She didn't like the unwanted stares from strangers but had learned to ignore them. As for any unwanted advances, she'd explain to the offending person that she was happy in her present relationship and would they kindly fuckoff. I had developed an appreciative awareness of Jackie's magnificent form but no longer let my eyes linger.

She insisted on being in the middle of everything going on as the medics prepared to get me onto a gurney. For my part I easily slipped into my "shut up and let the professionals do their job," mode. Other than my bloody nose, I really was not physically injured. I was just very tired and very dizzy. Standing up was not on the present menu.

The medics straightened me out so I was lying properly. The gurney was positioned on my right next to me. Jackie insisted on lifting my shoulders and head with the medics taking the heaver parts. The first attempt to lift me onto the gurney did not go well for my rescuers. For me it went very well.

Jackie was on her knees with her left arm under my shoulders and her right supporting my head. On the first attempt Jackie was not strong enough to lift the shoulders and just scooted my body sideways against the wheels of the gurney. As she did so the medics also stopped lifting and every one collapsed upon me.

Jackie's right breast was pushed right breast into my face and her left arm was now pinned under my left shoulder. As she rocked side to side to free her arm her breast kept pummeling my face. On one pummel her nipple was close to my mouth, so I moved my head and squeezed it with my lips. Jackie let out a squeak and reared back, looking into my face. I gave her my award wining shit-eating grin.

I may have lost the use of the left side of my body, but everything from the middle to the right still worked. At least until my upcoming aneurysm operation

Jackie, a Mona Lisa smile on her face, watched the medics get my bulk onto the gurney. As they were about to shove me into the ambulance, Jackie leaned over and gave me a quick kiss on the lips. As far as I was concerned, this ride was starting out a hell of a lot better than those in Costa Rica.

When the back doors to the ambulance closed, the medic riding in back with me said, "Your girl friend is very pretty."

"She's not my girl friend," I replied. "She's my neighbor."

"Any vacancies in your neighborhood?" he asked.

We were interrupted by the driver asking the medic which hospital they should take me to. They chose the one furthest from my house, and a sliver of doubt regarding the men's professionalism started forming in my head. I stopped talking and started wondering about what was next.

When we arrived at the emergency entrance of the too-far hospital, one of the suspect professionals yelled "surprise" when we rolled up to the nurses' station. The nurse in attendance did indeed look surprised. The place was old and dreary. Not as bad as Costa Rica, but close. I was used to the clean whiteness of the Seattle VA hospital. This place was marginal.

The ambulance medics wheeled me and my gurney into an examining room and shoved me onto a table while the nurse went to round up a doctor and orderly.

After a few minutes an old tired-looking doctor and scroungy-looking orderly arrived. I didn't feel really comfortable about being lying on a slab with these two in attendance. After a few questions from the doctor regarding what I was doing before I kissed the floor, he ordered the orderly to begin an IV drip of saline solution. According to him the gin and medicine I was taking had me dehydrated and I should eat more salt.

The orderly needed more practice because it hurt like hell when he jammed the needle into a vein in my right elbow. Thankfully he didn't need to go through that exercise with the second liter of water. The tube disconnected and the new bag clicked into place. It seemed to take longer with the second bag. I reasoned that I must be full and the rest was overflow that would have me up all night peeing when I got home.

When I was full the orderly pulled the needle out, plopped a cotton ball over the bleeding area, and held it in place with some tape. Then he helped me off the table and into the waiting area. The nurse behind the counter explained that she had called me a cab. This group of healthcare providers seemed to want me out of their hospital. I must bring out the best in all that I meet.

While waiting for my cab to arrive I surveyed the waiting area in front of the nurses' station. On the wall behind the counter was a large pegboard with tools hung on it, a hammer, a hacksaw, and a huge bolt-cutter among them. I asked the nurse what the bolt cutters were for.

"Taking off penis rings when the penis is infected," she replied.

Thankfully, my cab arrived before I found out what the hammer and hacksaw were used for. The mental image of a swollen penis with a metal ring through it was enough for one evening.

The cabbie helped me out to his cab and I struggled to get in the back seat as the front seat was pushed all the way back to make room for the teenage girls sitting in front. I don't know what they were doing when they received the call to pick me up, but the heater was going full blast and the windows were still fogged up.

When we returned to my house the cabbie helped me into my house where I found money to pay him. I wished him a very good night and climbed into bed.

I managed to stay upright for the next week or so, while the southern Oregon summer heat moved in. Jackie and I lived in two separate houses on one lot; Jackie's the front house, mine in back. Behind my house was a large grassy area for a garden or lawn games. I decided one Saturday that I needed to get out in the sun and work on my tan. Dressed in my best short shorts, I took a cooler of beer and a plastic lawn chair out to the back yard, using the lawn chair for a cane. I popped open a beer and leaned back in the chair enjoying the heat of the sun. As I have a very large mustache, I am sure I looked like a bloated white walrus in a plastic lawn chair. I must have been very handsome.

I had not seen or heard Jackie leave her house since my journey to the alternate hospital. I figured she had moved in with her boyfriend. She showed up just as I was starting to add an additional layer of sweat to my rapidly pinkening bloated body. Ever since my fall my balance was really out of whack, so I was afraid to take a shower. My last shower had been at the hospital in Seattle. I was at the point where I couldn't stand my body odor. I planned to try a sponge bath when I was finished ripening in the hot sun.

"What's in the cooler?" Jackie said, waking me from my odiferous reverie.

"Beer. You want one?" I replied, lifting the top of the cooler.

Our friendship had matured to the point where we understood each other so there was a refreshing directness in our interchanges. Jackie was wearing her at home uniform, short shorts and a T-shirt that she had cut off at the bottom so that it ended up falling just below her breasts. It was, as usual, a very skimpy sexy outfit. When she bent over to get a beer out of the cooler her butt was closer to me so she was bending away from me exposing the underside of her breasts. I stared opened mouthed. When she stood up and faced me I hadn't closed my mouth or recovered from my stare.

"Are you okay?" she asked.

"Jesus, Jackie. You're nude," I replied, as I regained a somewhat normal expression.

"No, I'm not," she replied as she looked down, brushing off what was left of the T-shirt with her non-beer hand.

"When you bent over I saw your boobs."

"You've seen them lots of times."

"No. I haven't," I said, still somewhat uncomfortable with all of this. I was starting to respond and was scared to do so.

Jackie faced me, placed her beer on the ground, stood upright and lifted her T-shirt exposing her chest. For my part in this erotic exchange, I resumed my slack open mouthed dumb look.

"Well, now you have," she said letting the shirt drop.

I could not respond as I was fighting a losing battle with the erection demon trying to break out of my shorts.

"Say something," she demanded.

I opened my legs and rammed my ice cold can of beer into my crotch sending my all too responsive demon back into his cage. I gestured at her with my one working hand and stammered.

"Jackie, you're beautiful."

The Mona Lisa smile I had seen when I was pushed into the ambulance returned. "Thank you," she said softly.

She sat down on the grass next to my chair and stretched out her legs. Raising both arms above her head in a sensuous feline manner, she said, "I love the sun. Don't you?"

"Yep."

"Is it like this in Costa Rica?"

"Yes, but not as hot," I said, intrigued by the exposed part of her boobs visible when she lifted her arms.

"I would love to see Costa Rica," she said. "You make it sound romantic."

"Well, come with me when I go down next," I said.

Her response was quick. "I will," she said. It was surprising, too, because she was in a long term relationship with a guy she referred to as Jimmy.

"What would Jimmy say?" I asked.

"Nothing," she replied.

Now I was really confused. If I had a girlfriend like Jackie, I'd be very uncomfortable if she went off to a foreign country, especially with someone like me.

"I don't understand," I said.

"We broke up."

"What?" I said, somewhat shocked. "When?"

"The day after you went to the hospital," she said in a soft voice.

"Why?" I asked.

"I think I've found someone I like better," she said, her voice sounding like a kitten's purr. My stomach felt funny, so I shut up and let the conversation drop.

We both were content to lie in the sun, quietly enjoying each others company without words to interfere. I was just about asleep when Jackie asked, "May I have another beer?"

"Sure," I said, as I scooted up in my chair, eyes wide open ready for another possible view of Jackie's breasts as she leaned over to get a beer out of the cooler. As luck would have it she positioned herself as she had before, her bottom close to my right shoulder as she leaned forward to open the cooler. When she did so a movement on her left calf caught my attention. A daddy longlegs spider was moving up her calf, almost to the inside of her knee. Recognizing that the spider was not poisonous, I placed the fingers of my right hand on her calf and slowly moved them up her smooth skin toward the spider. I wanted to get it to crawl onto my hand so I could get rid of it without harming it. The spider wanted nothing to do with my hand and continued upward. Slowly the spider and my hand continued up the smooth warm skin of the inside of her knee, moving toward the inside of her thigh. At this point I changed tactics and flipped the spider off Jackie's thigh. As I was concentrating on the spider, I sensed rather than saw that Jackie had stopped breathing. She slowly turned towards me and asked in her kitten purr voice, her eyes looking sleepy, "What are you doing?"

"Nothing." Again, my stomach was feeling funny. "You had a spider on your leg and I was trying to get it off you."

She turned towards me and leaned over, her face close to mine, and softly said, "Thank you."

Then she jerked her head back, a puzzled look on her face, and with a firm voice told me, "You need to take a shower. You stink!"

"When we finish the beer, I'm going to take a sponge bath," I replied.

"A sponge bath won't do it; you need to take a shower."

"Can't."

"What do you mean, can't?"

"I'm afraid of falling down in the shower."

"*What?*"

"Ever since I went to the hospital, I keep getting dizzy. So I can't take a chance with closing my eyes in the small shower I have."

"So you haven't had a shower since you fell on the floor?" she asked.

"I haven't had a shower since the VA hospital in Seattle."

"Jesus H. Christ! How did you shower at the VA?"

"The nurses helped, and there were waist height grab bars to steady me all around the shower stall."

"Can't you hold onto the cold or hot water handles?" she asked.

"I tried that and scalded myself. When I turn my bad arm turns also. It turned down the cold water and wouldn't let go. Trying to get out of the shower damn near killed me."

"There's nothing else for you to brace yourself with?"

"Only the bar across the opening at the top of the shower. I can only reach that with my good right arm."

Jackie was silent for a moment. Then, with a slow mischievous half smile, she said, "Okay, I'll shower you."

An instant "bullshit" was my response.

Her smile grew a tad larger, her eyes downcast. "Why not?" she asked.

"Because!"

"Because why?"

"You're my neighbor," was all I could come up with.

"The nurses helped you at the VA, and I'm a nurse. What's the difference?"

I was starting to feel strange, but in an uncomfortably good way. Like when you realize you are on the wrong side of an argument with a woman and she knows she's got you. I felt like she was the cat, and I was the mouse, and it would only be a matter of time. So I stammered the only thing I could think of, "I've seen your tits!"

"Oh, for Christ's sake," Jackie said, sitting back down on the grass next to my chair and taking a sip of beer.

I was, as they say, conflicted. I wanted the shower conversation to end and yet I knew the kitten sitting next to me was not through with her captive mouse. I jammed my cold beer into my crotch hoping it would close the dead bolt on the erection demon's cell.

Early on in my sexual education, an older lover had initiated me into the erotic slow dance of communal showers. The warm water, the sensual application of soap on you and your lovers body, the painful building of sexual tension, all of these memories started emerging as I closed my eyes in sweet reverie. The erection demon was starting to pick the lock on his cell and my beer was getting warmer.

My sweet memories were abruptly ended when I felt Jackie's cool hand on my warm thigh. As I opened my eyes to sit up I slapped her hand away.

"What the hell are you doing?" I stammered.

Jackie was pouting at my slapping her hand, but her eyes gave her away. The kitten was still playing with her mouse.

"Why won't you let me bathe you?" she asked.

"Jackie, please stop. I am old, fat, and embarrassed about my body."

"You have acanthosis, plus you'll get blackheads if

you don't get a good shower," she said, ignoring my feelings about my old body. She was not going to let go of the assisted shower idea. "I bathe old guys at the hospital all the time, why won't you let me help you?"

"Because we're friends," I said.

"That is precisely why you should let me help you."

"Shit" I said, wishing the kitten would just bite the head of the long suffering mouse and get it over with. Now the fond memories of long past communal showers had faded. I was clammy, sweaty, and stank. I needed a shower. "Okay."

My only experience with a woman helping me shower had been in Costa Rica and the VA hospital and those experiences were just business. But I really had nothing to worry about, right? Jackie was a nurse and would do a nurse's job. *No problemo* was my thinking at the moment.

"Good," Jackie said, getting to her feet. "Let's go."

"I gotta finish my beer," I said, delaying the inevitable.

Jackie stood over me with her hands on her hips, a slight smile as she watched me slowly down the last of my demon warmed beer.

I struggled out of the lawn chair and started to fold it up to use as my cane when Jackie asked, "What are you doing?"

"I'm getting ready to run away," I said. "I need this for my cane."

"Just use my shoulder," she said. "It will be much faster." She moved closer so I could rest my right hand on her left shoulder.

So off we went at a pace much too rapid for my semi dead left leg and after five or so steps I stumbled. In an effort to remain upright, I moved my hand to the back of Jackie's neck for a more secure hold. Jackie stopped and asked, "What are you doing?"

"You're going too fast and this is more secure," I said.

"Okay, I'll slow down. We can't have you falling. You might break something that actually works," she said, her eyelids a shade lower than normal.

We started off once again on our forty yard journey back to my house. After a few steps, I realized that I could relax my death grip on Jackie's neck, as the pace was one I could handle. Concentrating on moving my left leg in an orderly fashion, I subconsciously started lightly moving my hand up and down on her neck. Jackie stopped walking and turned slowly towards me.

"What are you doing?" she said.

"What? Nothing," I said. I genuinely had no idea what she was talking about.

"Your hand on my neck?"

"Oh," I said, and paused, thinking about what I had done. "Your skin is very smooth and I have not had contact with an attractive woman in a very long time. I'm sorry. I didn't mean to startle you."

"Oh, okay. Let's go," she said. Her eyes looked as if she was tired.

For the third time we started off. I was now concentrating on two very important items. My left leg's movement and Jackie's creamy smooth neck. She had not told me to stop. The beers and the medicine I was taking had slowed me down, both physically and mentally. My hand on her neck moved slowly up the outside until my fingers were lightly moving behind her ear. Then, in a relaxed fog, I moved my fingers down until they rested on her collar bone underneath her T-shirt. In a lazy motion I moved my fingers underneath the fabric out towards her shoulder. Our pace had slowed to a point that I could spend more time enjoying my caresses of Jackie's neck than concentrating on walking.

Somewhere in my dysfunctional mind a dim bulb started to glow brighter. I had moved from two friends enjoying each others company to the slight sexual tension of a man trying to seduce a woman. The light was bright enough for me to barely recognize what was going on, but not bright enough as yet to wake the erection demon. Our pace had slowed to almost a standstill when Jackie said, "I like the way you are tickling me."

"Your skin is so silky smooth," I said, "But I am caressing your neck, not tickling it."

"Whatever you colonials call it, I will give you two hours to stop it," Jackie said, once again starting to move forward.

"It's going to take two hours to get to the house?" I asked.

"Jesus, you take things literally," she said as she quickened our pace.

I went back to enjoying the feel of Jackie's smooth skin and concentrating on remaining upright. As we reached the two steps leading up to the deck by my front door, Jackie had a handrail to hold onto but I didn't. Because of this, I stopped my caressing and strengthened my hold of her neck. Jackie stumbled, and I followed. It was a case of each of us trying to help the other but as a result we both toppled forward, grabbing for the other. We didn't really fall; we just sort of leaned forward onto the deck.

We ended up lying on the deck, our faces inches from each other. Jackie had a hand under me; I had a hand on her breast. When I realized where my hand was I awkwardly yanked it away.

"Jesus, I'm sorry," I said. "I didn't mean to grab your boob. Are you okay?"

"Yes, I'm okay. You men are all alike, always trying to feel up a woman."

I must have had a guilty look on my face that got her giggling. I soon joined in as we lay face to face. When we stopped laughing, Jackie once again got a funny look on her face and kissed me on the lips. Just like when I was being loaded into the ambulance, only a little longer and a little more open mouthed.

"Does that mean you forgive me for grabbing your boob?" I asked, while enjoying the memory of her lips and the soft feel of her breast.

"So you did grab me on purpose?" she said.

"No, no," I responded quickly.

"That's okay. I kind of liked it. Let's get in the house, you still need a shower."

I was really confused as we struggled to our feet and into the house.

Once inside I focused on what was about to happen and started feeling both fear and excitement about the possibilities of what we were about to do.

"You go get undressed while I get the shower going," Jackie ordered like the nurse she was. I had made it into the bedroom by leaning onto the walls.

"Jackie," I said. "I can't do this."

She came into the bedroom and stood over me as I sat on the edge of the bed.

"What is the problem now?" she wanted to know.

"I really feel uncomfortable about this."

"Don't worry, I'll be gentle and respect you in the morning," was her flippant response.

"Stop it," I said quickly. "I am serious."

"I'm sorry," she said and sat down next to me on the bed. "Please explain."

I was about to ruin my friendship with this beautiful young woman. But it had to be done. I took a deep breath and started out on what I thought would be the most uncomfortable statement I had made since before my stroke. I made sure I had her attention by making and holding eye contact.

"Jackie, I think you are a wonderful person."

"Are we breaking up?" she interrupted.

"Let me finish before you respond, okay?"

"Okay."

"Now, where was I?"

"You were telling me I was a wonderful person," she prompted.

I started again. "Jackie, you are a wonderful person, and if I had a daughter, I would want her to be exactly like you."

"But I'm not your daughter," she interrupted again.

"Let me finish," I said, a little more forcefully.

"Okay," she said, with an exaggerated pout and maintaining eye contact.

"Yes, you are not my daughter. And that's what makes it difficult. I think you are intelligent, beautiful, sexy, sensual, and you have a body that dirty old men like me fantasize about."

"Thank you."

"Stop it! Let me finish!"

"Okay." This time there was a slight smile in her pout.

"I am old, overweight, and have an ugly body. But I am really scared I might respond in an inappropriate manner if you help me shower, and—"

"You're worried you'll get an erection," she stated.

"Yes. And stop interrupting," I said, and then realized I had no more to say. So I just shut up.

After a slight pause, Jackie asked, "Is it my turn?"

"Yes."

"Okay. You are not my father, and for that I am grateful. My father was a miserable bastard. I am pleased you find me attractive. I am a nurse and part of my job is helping dirty old men, such as yourself, shower. Some of them actually do get erections. So I am used to seeing the penis erect. Although it might be fun to see yours," she finished, using that half smile that scared me.

"You were doing fine until the last part," I said. "Look. I am recovering from a stroke, I have an aneurysm that is about to explode, I can hardly stand upright, and I fall a lot."

"First, you are not going to fall. I looked at the

shower and saw that you can hold onto the top of the walls. Second, you would not be allowed out of the hospital if you were at any significant risk. So stop stalling and get your old butt into the shower." She got up and went into the bathroom.

When I heard the water running I realized that I was going to take a shower. Her old butt comment moved my thinking from seduction to business. This was nothing erotic, just a shower with help from my neighbor. I removed my clothes and, holding onto the walls, made it into the bathroom.

Jackie was pouring shampoo into her hand as I entered my bathroom and moved into the shower, my back towards her.

"I take it back," she said. "You have a cute butt."

I turned to face her. She had a large smile pasted on her face. We were back to being just friends. I felt more comfortable.

Jackie explained that we would start at the top and work our way down.

When she had me stick my head under the water, I expected a vigorous scrubbing like at the hospital. All business. What I got was a slow massage of my head and neck.

"You can go faster," I said. "Let's get this over with."

"I'm the nurse, I'm in charge. Now turn and rinse the shampoo out," she ordered.

As I slowly turned into the water, Jackie said, "Hey, watch it."

"I can't see a thing, my eyes are closed," I said as the water stream hit me on the top of my head.

"You did it again," Jackie said.

When I felt like the shampoo was out of my hair, I turned toward Jackie and opened my eyes. The front of her T-shirt was sopping wet. She could win any wet T-shirt contest she entered. I started laughing, she quickly followed. She turned serious and threatened me. "I'll get you for that."

Behind my world famous shit-eating grin, I said, "Oh dear, now I'm really scared."

"Get your face wet; it's next," she ordered. "And try not to soak me again."

I did as ordered and she was sprayed again. She had turned when she saw the water coming so this time it was her side and part of her back that got it.

"I might as well climb in the shower with you," she said. "I'm soaking wet."

"There's not enough room," I said.

"Okay. Hold still while I wash your face."

I closed my eyes and once again it was the gentle touch rather than the businesslike scrub that I'd expected. When ordered to rinse off my face I did so. I turned and faced Jackie. She took hold of my semi-dead left wrist and slowly rubbed the bar of soap all over my arm, down my side, and around to my bottom. I sensed that she was enjoying herself at my expense, but before I could say anything she moved up to my neck. Then she started rubbing the soap across my chest in a slow, sensuous, swaying motion. I had closed my eyes, enjoying the gentle caresses of the soap and her hand across my body.

By the time she had reached my lower stomach, that

dim bulb in the dark recesses of my mind was burning brightly and my demon was dancing, so pleased with his proud self.

Like all males I enjoyed my condition but I was concerned that I didn't offend Jackie. I opened my eyes and said, "I hope this doesn't offend you?"

"What are you talking about?" she said. "I'm flattered and very impressed." Her eyes were wide open in mock astonishment. "Now rinse yourself off, turn around, and we will do your back."

I gladly did as ordered. Jackie continued her slow washing of my back. When she started on my butt, I thought she was having too much fun with her work. Her slow movements might be getting me clean, but they were definitely getting me more aroused.

She started washing my legs, reaching around in front but stopping short of my personal demon. By the time she made the same movements with my other leg I desperately didn't want her to stop short of anything. I had trouble breathing with the sweet pain my demon was sharing with me. My back towards her, Jackie moved her hand between my legs, moving towards the front of my body.

"Whoa," I fairly shouted. "Jackie, please don't."

"We need to wash this part too."

"You're not playing fair," I said weakly, my breathing labored.

"All is fair in love and war," she replied as she repeated her move, more slowly this time.

"God help me," I prayed softly.

At that Jackie returned to her nurse demeanor.

"Okay, rinse yourself off, get out, and let me dry you off."

I did as I was told and stood tall, touching the wall for support as Jackie quickly dried me off. I was aroused to the point of pain, something I had not felt since my teenage and twenty-something years. I was ready to explode and felt shaky standing up.

Nurse Jackie said, "You look like you need to lie down. Hold on to my neck and we'll get you into bed."

We started off towards the bedroom with my right hand cradling Jackie's neck. About the third step we took, the natural movement of our bodies had Jackie's left hand smack the demon. I stopped. Jackie smiled up at me and grabbed the demon erection.

"What are you doing?" I said.

"If you don't know by now, you're dumber than a rock," was the reply.

She moved closer with her head on my chest. We started off again, Jackie choking the demon, me not breathing.

When we reached the bed room I was close to delirium, unable to speak. I really wasn't that dumb. Jackie maneuvered me using the demon as one would use the tongue of a trailer to position it where you wanted. In my case it was my legs up against the bed. Jackie said

"Sit"

I sat. Jackie then bent over and grabbed my legs, swinging them onto the bed.

"Scoot."

I did as told and scooted further away from the edge.

Jackie stood looking at my prostrate form and its crazed demon looking around for a friend. She slowly pulled her wet T-shirt over her head and dropped it to the floor. I could only gulp and silently pray for what I hoped would be next. She unhooked her shorts and let them join the T-shirt on the floor. I had never seen such pure beauty. A natural blond woman standing nude beside me. I was so aroused that I had difficulty focusing. Not good at a time like this.

"Where are your condoms?" Jackie asked.

"I don't have any," I whispered.

"What?"

"I said I don't have any," I said, feeling the opportunity about to slip away.

Jackie stood over me just looking at my helplessness for a long long time and said, "Bloody hell!"

With that, she climbed on the bed and straddled me just above the pleading demon. At this point I was incapable of speech or rational thought. Jackie had her sexy half smile back as she slowly lowered herself onto me. I moaned as she took me fully. We stayed like this motionless for a few seconds while Jackie adjusted to me.

She started to rock forward and I squeezed my muscles controlling the demon so he would not explode too soon.

Jackie started moving up and down as the emotional and physical pleasure in me grew to a point where it could no longer be controlled. I thrust upward with my orgasm in blinding white light. Jackie let out a high pitched squeak, bending forward to give me an open mouth kiss as my spasms continued to subside. We lay together reveling in the love and peace our actions had created.

I felt the same overwhelming peace and love that I had experienced during my out of body journey during my stroke.

Suddenly Jackie sat upright and looked at me in a quizzical way.

"You're cute," she said. "What's your name again?"

I laughed and drew her back down on me with a one arm hug.

The next thing I was aware of was I was having difficulty breathing. There were a few seconds of panic until I opened my eyes and found Jackie asleep on top of me, both of us still connected to the other. We'd fallen asleep from our exertions. I moved my hips and fell out of Jackie. She let out a soft moan and opened her eyes.

She sat up and said, "Thanks, I needed that."

I replied, "I more so than you." I recalled my fear in the hospital of never making love to a woman again.

We acted like teenagers during the next week or so, constantly caressing each other. We couldn't keep our hands off, nor stop a constant flow of love words.

I would wake up before Jackie, make coffee and bring a cup to her while she was still in bed. She would leave for work and I would start on dinner. Before my stoke, when I had two hands that worked, I was an accomplished cook. With only one hand and a not too stable body, I needed more time to cook the evening meal. When Jackie came home from work, I would have a glass of her favorite wine ready. We would sit on the deck sipping our wine while Jackie told me about her day. After the wine, I would serve Jackie the meal I had concocted during the day. After the meal we would watch a movie on TV or go out for a drive. We acted as If we had been together forever. We both expressed our enjoyment of what we had.

For me, there was one great difference, the feelings I felt were so deep, so awe inspiring, I could not at first trust them. As a person with life experiences I tried to logically associate my feeling with previous experiences. When I realized that the emotions I felt with this woman were more intimate than anything in the past, I just went with the moment.

We talked for hours on end. I was pleased with the honesty we shared. Nothing was off limits. We shared our darkest fears, our most fervent hopes and desires. I learned that intimate caresses did not need to end in physical climax, that intimacy was a goal in itself.

The only fear I had was that I was acting like an old fool. The background noise of this thinking had me worrying about the possibility that all of this would end. Then, an epiphany; I had not worried about having a stroke that could kill me or an aneurysm that could accomplish the same thing. Shit happens. So I stopped the negative bullshit and fell into deep, complete, unconditional love. With this acceptance of my love for this woman came a peace of being I never knew existed.

Jackie and I talked about my upcoming operation and my chances of survival. Because of her profession, she had had experience with patients who had gone through this procedure. At first, she acted as if there was nothing to it. Then, one night while we were lying in bed enjoying the glow of our lovemaking, she admitted that she was afraid. She told me that while she knew that the odds were in my favor, she did not want to lose me. I told her not to worry, that I had tried dying once and screwed it up so I wasn't going to die in a couple of weeks. Secretly the possibility lingered in my mind.

Three days before I was to leave for Seattle for my operation Jackie came home just before noon crying. Her parents in England had been in a car accident after which her father had suffered a heart attack. Her mother had a broken leg, broken ribs, and internal bleeding. She had to return home.

Because it was the height of tourist season, try as she might she could not get a flight out of Portland for two days. I suggested that she try leaving out of Seattle. If she could get out sooner I could drive up early and deliver her to the airport. She got booked on a flight for the next evening and I called my son and told him to expect me a day early, which was not a problem.

Jackie went to her house and started packing. I wandered over later to see how she was doing. We agreed that I'd sell her car and send the money to her in England and empty the house of her furniture and belongings, store them in my garage, and notify the rental agency of her leaving.

That evening Jackie spent over an hour talking to her elderly aunt in England. From her reaction to the conversation, I could tell the news was not good. Her father was in intensive care and her mother was in the operating room.

Like most of the intense situations I had experienced, time slowed down. The evening dragged on each of us in our private thoughts. Jackie I was sure was trying to think of all she needed to remember, plus imagining the possible scenarios she might endure once she arrived home. I was frustrated because no matter how hard I thought about the situation, I realized there was nothing I could do to protect and comfort her. She would be on her own.

We spent most of the night not sleeping but holding each other. Jackie finally fell asleep around three in the morning. I ended up staying awake the entire night.

The next morning I got up while she was still sleeping, made the coffee and took her a cup. I kissed her on her forehead to wake her and gave her the coffee. She took it and started crying when she realized that this was not a normal morning.

I took the cup and placed it on the floor. Then I climbed into bed and held her until she stopped crying. We dressed in silence. When she was ready, I carried our bags out to the car while she locked up my house.

This trip north to Seattle was different for me, anxious and depressing. I was driving through those same Siskeyou Mountains I'd enjoyed on my release from the hospital. The mountains were no longer vibrant new green with springtime growth, but the dull green of leaves suffering their last in a hot summer day. I was heading north to repair the aneurysm that was my personal ticking bomb and delivering the woman I loved to an uncertain future.

The problem was that the glass once half full of hope was now overflowing with apprehensive dread. My joy in being alive was gone, replaced with the cold knowledge that someone was going to slit me open from my sternum to my dick and go play rock, scissors, paper with my guts. What was even more disquieting was I was willingly going to the party. All of this magnified by the possibility that I was going to lose the most precious woman I had ever known.

As I drove north on I-5 Jackie and I talked about what we each were facing. Crying, she explained her fear of losing her parents. For my part I shared Morin's warning of never getting assigned to the third floor of pain, which was exactly where the letter of instruction for my procedure had instructed me to go. We all are anxious about, if not afraid of, the unknown. Add to that fear the certain knowledge that the end of your life is a possible part of the equation and it makes for an unsettling ride. On this trip north I was not the joyful person I had been upon my release from the hospital some months before, no longer excited with seeing the world anew. Now it was just the cold reality of modern life filled with personal obligations and the joyful commitment to this woman sitting beside me.

I was exhausted after staying awake all night. This exhaustion shredded the last of my emotional barriers and I gently told Jackie, "I love you."

"I know," she replied. "It took you long enough to realize it."

"Give me a break," I said. "I just told you I love you."

"I fell in love with you the night of the gurney."

"Wow," I said. "I really was behind the power curve."

"So what should we do now?" she asked.

"How would you like to spend the rest of your life with a dirty old man who will adore you until the day he dies?"

"I can't answer that," Jackie said, and started crying.

"Why not?" I asked, shocked.

"Because of what's about to happen to us both," she sobbed.

"Reality rears its ugly head," I said, as I started to cry also.

We were just north of Tacoma a few minutes from the airport, both of us crying with our understanding of the fate we both faced.

"When we get to the terminal I am going to just jump out," Jackie said. "I do not want a long goodbye. Okay?"

"Okay," I said as bravely as I could through my tears.

I took the airport exit as we both sat crying. When we were almost to the terminal I suddenly realized that in our rushing around I did not have a phone number for Jackie in England.

"Jackie, quick," I demanded. "Give me a number where I can reach you."

As we slowed to the curb at the terminal, Jackie

pulled out a small notebook she had in her purse and started writing. A cop directing traffic motioned us to get moving. Jackie asked for my son's phone number when the cop tapped the window with his night club. I gave her my son's number and she jumped out of the car, opened the back door, grabbed her bag and disappeared in the people rushing about. The cop gave me one more tap on the window and I moved out into traffic. When I had left the airport and was heading to I-5 I realized that I did not have a way to contact Jackie. I started sobbing.

I was still crying when I swung the car off the five onto the off-ramp leading to the West Seattle bridge at forty-five miles an hour. That had been the previously posted speed. As I finished driving the gentle curve of the ramp onto the bridge ascent I was joined by blue flashing lights in my rear view mirror.

Two days before my arrival at this graceful curve a mother and three children had been killed when a semi had taken the same curve too fast. The semi could not stay in the appointed lane and swung into the merging traffic hitting the woman's car and killing the occupants. In a well intentioned move of political brilliance, the mayor of Seattle had seized upon the tragedy to prove he was keeping a campaign promise to clean up the streets. The posted speed was now twenty five miles an hour. There was no leeway. Speeders like me would get a speeding ticket with a disproportionately high fine.

Adding to the impending financial pain was the embarrassment of no place to hide on the on ramp to the bridge and my devastation on losing Jackie. There I was, crying, blocking a lane of traffic, blue lights advertising the fact that I was possibly some serial killer, of which Seattle could boast such examples as Ted Bundy and the Green River killer. Cars drove by slowly by so that the drivers could catch a glimpse of the psychotic miscreant that the valiant police officer, slowly sauntering up to the car with his right hand on the butt of his pistol, was apprehending. Imagine all of this and you have a life altering event, definitely not mood enhancing for the difficulties to come.

I carry my driver's license in a small leather credit card holder. Because I only had one hand working, it felt like it took me fifteen minutes to get it out for the kind office who neither smiled nor removed his hand from the butt of his gun. During this time several cars honked as they passed, either to support the brave officer or to show their displeasure with where I had stopped to block traffic. This type of exposure had me sinking lower in my seat until I was looking through the steering wheel at the road way in front of the car. I was ashamed of my crying. The officer noticed but went about his business without comment. After I graciously accepted his request for my autograph I was sent on my way. I didn't know it at the time, but this was going to be as good as it would get over the next several weeks.

Dinner that evening with my son's wife and child was a subdued feast of delivery pizza and beer. I took my medicine with the yellow warning labels about alcohol consumption with a cold India Pale Ale. After an hour or so and two more beers coupled with the drugs provided by the hospital, I slowly slipped into a relaxed state. Screw it, I did not care if I lived or died. Now I was ready for the next day.

WELCOME HOME CEREMONY

The next day my son again took time off from his job to drive me and my government-issue wheelchair to the hospital. The instructions I had been sent told me to report to the West wing of the third floor. My son and I said our goodbyes at the front door and I wheeled myself into a new adventure.

I'd been instructed to report by three in the afternoon. At three minutes before three, I wheeled myself up to the admissions desk as ordered. The clerk sitting behind the desk did not look up but asked me my name and social security number. Without looking at me he kept typing, and then informed me that I was in the wrong spot and to report to the East wing. As I wheeled around to leave I caught a glimpse of his computer screen. Whatever game he was playing had just told him he had been killed. That was just fine by me.

There was a long hallway between the East and West wings and, while wheeling myself along it, I was met by a nurse who asked if she could help me. I told her that the last guy I had seen had told me I was supposed to go to the East wing, and handed her the instructions I had received in the mail. She read them and muttered something under her breath. I could have been wrong but it sure sounded like "asshole." That was fine by me also.

"Follow me," she said and off we went heading westward. When we arrived at the West wing admissions desk, Asshole was nowhere to be found. Another clerk was at the desk and explained that Asshole had had to leave early. The new clerk took the letter from the nurse and thanked her for bringing the wayward Patient back to where he belonged. I was checked in, given a wristband that I couldn't remove no matter how hard I tried, and a nurse was summoned to wheel me to my room.

When we got there, the nurse instructed me to get undressed and said she would bring me a gown. I asked for a strapless, but she didn't laugh. She was all business. She returned in less than two minutes with my gown and two large containers of liquid which I was told I had to drink before the evening was out. When I asked what this was for, I was told it was to clean out my system. I had a very busy afternoon drinking and running to the bathroom.

Dinner that evening consisted of a ton of Jell-o and bland baby food. After dinner a nurse arrived with a small paper cup containing several pills. I was instructed to take the pills while she observed my swallowing procedure. When through, I had to open my mouth and lift up the tongue to make sure all the pills had been swallowed. I passed the test.

The pills took effect in about thirty minutes, making me sleepy. Later, while I was dozing, another nurse arrived and gave me several shots.

The next morning was an absolute blur. I think it went like this; I was shaken awake by two big guys and thrown on a gurney. At some point in the rush a stint was stuck into the vein in my left arm. By the time we arrived at the prep area I was almost out. I was surprised to see that the gurney next to me held a woman. I didn't think much of it as I had taken my army induction physical with girls who were to become WACS. But that is another story. The next thing was a tube up through my nose and down to my stomach. As this was going on, someone stuck a needle containing clear liquid into the stint in my left arm, pushed the plunger down, and I went out.

I came back to earth to the sound of a female voice telling me, "I am going to pull this tube out. Okay?"

Before I could respond she gave a yank and the tube that was in my throat came out. Like my regaining consciousness the first time after my stroke, everything was confusing, and most of me did not work. Unlike coming to in the Costa Rican hospital however, there were no songs on the radio. Just my son's voice. "Hi dad, how you doing?"

After a few moments of small talk, I fell asleep until the evening. I awoke to hear a male voice screaming, "Motherfuckers, give me my meds."

The third floor curse that Morin had warned me about so many months before was true. This was too much to handle, so I went back to sleep.

The next morning had a slow groggy feel. None of the nurses I had met so far on the third floor knew how to smile and the one who broke through the morning fog this morning was no different. No nonsense efficiency with a paper cup of pills and a syringe. The pills in the cup routine was the same; pills in mouth, examine paper cup to assure all went into mouth, examination of mouth to assure all the pills had started their journey towards the stomach.

"Lift your gown up above your stomach," was the greeting offered. No "Good morning," no "How are you doing today?"

Even in Spanish words that I didn't understand, the greetings in the Costa Rican hospital were significantly more warm and real.

"Why do you want to see my stomach?" I asked. I hadn't seen my own stomach since I went out in pre-op. So I added to the question, "If you show me yours, I will show you mine." That got me a rude stare and a "lift your gown."

So I lifted my gown and discovered someone had put a zipper in my stomach. It wasn't just my stomach; it started at my sternum and wandered down and around my belly button, ending at my dick. Nice shiny stainless steel staples every inch or so to hold the parted sides of my body together. While I was still trying to understand my new zipper the nurse rubbed my belly with a cotton ball dripping with cold alcohol.

"Hold it. What are you doing?" I said, moving my only good hand over the cold spot on my belly to protect it.

"Giving you an injection. Move your hand," was the answer to my question.

"What kind of injection do you get in the stomach?" I said. "Do I have rabies?"

"You don't have rabies. This is a blood thinner and it is given in the stomach," was her cool response.

"Could we move it to my arm instead?" I asked.

Without responding, the nurse raised my sleeve, swabbed my right arm near my shoulder with alcohol, gave me a rapid shot of blood thinner, and turned and left the room.

Alone with a stinging spot in my right shoulder I

took a peek at my new surroundings, another four bed room but without the TVs. There was a black guy in the bed next to mine and an empty bed opposite me. The fourth bed had a body that was covered up to its dark hairline and which didn't move much.

I said good morning to the black guy and he responded in kind.

"Were you here last night?" I asked him.

"Yes," he said. "You were kind of out of it. Was that big guy your son?"

"Yes. Did he yell mother fucker?" I asked.

"No, that's some crazy asshole. He's been doing that every evening since I've been here. When his drugs wear off he goes postal and starts yelling all kinds of shit."

"How long you been here."

"Two days. I get out this afternoon," he said, obviously relieved.

From his response I realized that Morin hadn't been bullshitting. The third floor was not a place to loiter.

Around three that afternoon we were joined by a rather stout individual and his equally stout wife. He was placed in the empty bed directly in front of me and introductions were made. His name was Fred, and his wife's was Jan. I learned he was to be cut open the next morning to repair a titanium ladder that held his spine in place. Unlike me, he did not appear to have any reservation regarding his upcoming operation, as this was his second try. Evidently the preceding open body experience did not take.

After Fred's wife had left, another dour but efficient

nurse arrived with the two large bottles of liquid to clean out his radiator and other parts of his chassis. Fred started taking large swigs of the body cleaner-outer as if he actually liked the stuff. When he had swallowed all he could handle at one drinking, he smiled, demonstrated his body control, and expelled a good twenty-second belch.

"God damn, that stuff tastes like turtle shit," he said.

"I thought it could gag a maggot," was my reply. "Look at the bright side; you'll be clean as a tin whistle when they cut you open."

"Just trying to support our troops and make the world safe for democracy," he said.

We talked for a while then settled back into hospital silence. This type of silence occurs when room mates with nothing more in common but their incarceration run out of things to say. At that point we retreat into our own thoughts about our present condition, our families and our mortality.

Later that afternoon, two nurses arrived, each with a paper cup and a syringe. My shot was the blood thinner that I had persuaded the previous nurse to give me in my upper right arm in lieu of my stomach. I have no idea how this nurse knew about it, but she plugged it into the arm without asking. Now the mildly sore area really hurt.

That evening, just after Fred and I had finished our evening meal, the quiet was interrupted by a shout of "Where are my meds, you fucking whores?"

"Jesus," said Fred, a startled look on his face. "What's going on out there?"

"Just some crazy fucker," I replied. "He does that sort of yelling, but only on a full stomach and at this time every night. Get used to it."

"I want my meds," said Fred.

Both of our evening medicines arrived shortly after the third floor yeller got his. Both of the paper cups had strong sedatives that had us both sleeping soundly within an hour.

When I awoke the next morning, Fred's bed was empty. Fred had had his spine squashed while serving in Nam unloading crates from the back of a truck. A large crate, that should have had additional personnel to offload it, fell on poor Fred and seriously screwed up his spine. When he had gone on sick call because of the pain, he was accused of goldbricking, or goofing off to get out of work. After several weeks of pain, an opening for the X-ray machine use for non combat personnel finally allowed the doctors to take a peek at Fred's mangled spine. Within a few seconds of their discovery, the doctors shoved Fred into the VA system, medical discharge and all. So now he was getting an adjustment to the titanium ladder that kept his spine in place. I think I was better off. All I had was a metal zipper in my gut.

That afternoon, as I was getting my blood thinner shot in the sore bump on my right shoulder, three large men in the baggy blue pajamas that signified that they were hospital important wheeled a gurney into the room with a sleeping Fred wrapped in a white sheet. For a moment I thought it might be a replay of the mortality play I had watched in the Costa Rican hospital. The blue clad men just slid Fred onto his bed, covered him with a new age space blanket that was supposed to keep you warm, and left. So I lay there shivering under my new age space blanket and waited for Fred to open his eyes. When he did finally decide to rejoin the world, he slowly sat up and declared that he was thirsty. I hit my nurse's call button on the side of the bed, but nothing happened. For an hour or so Fred would ask for water and we would both hit our call buttons to summon anybody available to get parched Fred some water. During this time the crazy guy broke loose again, screaming at the nurses that they were all some sort of unique slut and charged too little for their sexual services. Fred and I were used to the guy by now so we just ignored the commotion.

Finally a tall black nurse dressed in blue pajamas came in, looked around the room, and asked "Which one of you hit the call button?"

Both Fred and I raised our hand to speak. She pointed at me, so I pointed at Fred, who pointed at her and asked, in a raspy dry voice, "Could you please get me a glass of water?"

"Get it yourself, this is not a hotel," was her rude response.

"I know," replied Fred, proving he was indeed back with the living. "It is a hospital."

"Maybe you should have gone to a different hospital" said the rude blue pajama nurse and left our room.

"What the fuck just happened?" said a very thirsty Fred, feeling his tongue slowly starting to swell from the lack of water.

With that we both started to hit our call buttons.

It took a minute before another nurse, this one dressed in white, arrived and asked us what we wanted.

"Water!" we replied in unison. For some reason all of this water discussion had made me thirsty also.

"Okay, I'll be right back," she said, and left.

Because of the drugs I was taking it seemed like the room was filling and emptying at a rapid rate. It filled again when the white dressed nurse returned with two carafes of water and a glass for each of us. So I had one glassful while Fred not only emptied his glass but, like drinking out of a pitcher of beer, used the carafe to finish off the rest. He looked over at me with a peaceful look.

"Don't fuck with the nurses in blue," he said.

It was all too much excitement for me. I dozed off until I was awakened for dinner.

Along with dinner came Jan, Fred's wife. She had been unable to get off work to be there when Fred had come out of the operation, so she was pleased to see her husband sitting up and coherent. She asked all the questions a loving spouse would and Fred patiently answered them all. At one point Fred mentioned that he had run into a tiny blip when he was thirsty.

With that, all hell broke loose. Jan stormed out of the room confronting the first hospital person she ran into and demanded to know, "Just what the hell is going on?"

"Lady, I just deliver the meals," said the scared wide eyed orderly. "Try the nurse's station."

With a soft "Oh, shit," Fred went back to eating his meal.

For some reason all of this was starting to seem normal to me. The medicines I was taking were designed to keep me calm and were quite good at the task. So I hardly noticed Jan return with two nurses in tow and only looked up when I realized everyone was looking at me.

"What?" I said, slowly getting back into the present. I had completely blocked out the conversation they'd been having with Fred.

"Is that true?" asked one of the nurses, pointing at Fred.

"I guess," I replied. "What are we talking about?"

"The water," all three of the ladies replied.

"Yep," I said. "You don't mess with the nurses in blue."

Again, this was too much excitement for one day so I went into my personal zone, tuned them out, and fell asleep with only half of my dinner eaten.

The next morning, as I was getting another blood thinner shot in the now hard spot where the other injections had been given, the Patient Rep for the hospital arrived. I pointed to a dozing Fred and said, "He is the one you want to talk to."

"Hey Fred, you have company," I called, loud enough to get his eyes open.

I feigned indifference as Fred recounted his encounter with the blue clad nurse but, once he'd finished, it was my turn in the barrel.

Turning to face me, the Rep asked, "Were you present when all of this occurred?"

"I am not allowed out of bed until the doctor says so," was my response.

"So?"

"So...what?"

There was a long pause by the Rep while she registered that I was being a small problem. "Did you see what happened?" she eventually said.

"Sure did."

"And?"

This time I was sure she would wait for my response, so I responded. "And it happened just like Fred said it did."

"Thank you both, I will let you know what happens," the Rep said, leaving Fred and I alone with our drug induced thoughts.

A few days later, just before Fred was due to return home and I had been allowed out of bed, the Rep returned with some papers, a formal complaint, for Fred and me to sign. As we were reading the official BS in the complaint, the Rep said, "She was out of line no matter what."

"What do you mean, 'No matter what'?" Fred asked.

I stopped reading to concentrate on her answer.

"Well, she was tired after two shifts in the OR. She's a surgical nurse."

"Why did she work so long?" I asked

"Some kind of an emergency came up and we were understaffed, so she volunteered."

"Why was she on our floor?" Fred asked.

"She came to see if she could get a ride home with one of the floor nurses."

"And while she was doing that some crazy fucker called her a whore," I said.

"Yes, some crazy guy called her a whore," the rep said with a resigned attitude.

"So she was just trying to be helpful when she came in here?" Fred asked.

"Yes, that's about it."

"I'm not signing nothing," said Fred, and he held out the paperwork.

"Me neither," I added.

"Thank you, gentlemen," said the Rep as she collected the papers. "You did the right thing."

We both thought so also.

Fred must have been on steroids because he left for home before I could get the stainless steel zipper in my stomach removed. When the third floor became congested with recovering patients, I was sent to the first floor hospice to continue my recovery. All the rooms here were two bed rooms with their own bathrooms. My room faced one of the fairways of the neighboring golf course so the view out of the windows was really pleasant. Unfortunately there was a gentleman from Puerto Rico occupying the coveted window bed so I was in a short bed next to a blank wall off the bathroom.

Fernando, the gentleman from Puerto Rico, helped me with my Spanish and we promised to remain lifelong friends when he went home two days after I arrived. My only trip to the Island had been on a company trip to reward me for selling computers in my previous life before I became a professional hospital patient and owner of a coveted window bed.

My first night of sleep in this special bed was difficult for two major reasons. The first was due to my length, which again exceeded the length of the bed, so I was forced to sleep in a semi-fetal position. The metal zipper in my gut really did not bend the way I wanted, so periods of sleep were momentary and few.

The second reason for my sleep deprivation was because I started to have a disturbing dream regarding my open body operation. This dream was like a soap opera on TV. Each moment of sleep would have an advancing portion of the full story. This nocturnal drama continued for several days until I had a chance meeting with the staff psychiatrist who had talked to me on my first visit before my operation. The psychiatrist was a short black woman wearing a colorful dashiki. We had discussed the emotional reactions to a stroke assault. She had explained how my stroke would make me more emotional.

This meeting was accidental. The old folks' area had a small physical therapy room that I was using to try to continue my recovery. One morning on my way to the PT room in my wheelchair she stopped me in the hallway and asked me how things were going.

"The whole world hates me," was my reply.

"That's normal," she said. "You probably felt that way when you first realized you were paralyzed."

"You mean James wasn't trying to sell my farm out from under me?"

"What are you talking about?" she asked, as she took control of my wheelchair and pushed me over to a set of padded benches in an open area of the old folks' area lobby.

I explained how in the days shortly after my stroke I had thought that everyone was not working to help me but instead planning my death and the sale of my assets.

"No, no, no," she said. "This is a normal response. It is another version of the 'why me?' response. You do not really understand what's happening, and feel there must be a reason other than 'shit happens', something that makes sense to you. So a form of paranoia sets in and you look for the negative. When you can't find it, you look at your friends and loved ones and blame them for your pain."

"Shit," I said. "I was really into hating James. You

mean he was really looking to help me?"

"Absolutely," she responded. "You feel better now?"

"No, the world still hates me," I said.

"Okay, just why does the world hate you?"

"My bed is too short and I can't sleep."

Her dashiki covered shoulders slumped. "*What?*"

"I haven't really slept since I got here and I'm having painful dreams about my operation," I explained, telling her that I had repeatedly asked for a longer bed but no one had listened to me.

"The short bed sounds like discrimination to me," she said with a tone of profound understanding.

I had never considered this viewpoint until that moment. At six feet five inches tall, I had indeed experienced discrimination, ranging from too-small airplane seats to trying to find size fourteen shoes. Until this moment I had taken these sorts of things as slight annoyances rather than discrimination against overweight, tall old people. Just then James turned into a good guy. Instead of James, I now had something real to direct my anger towards.

"What about the painful dreams?" she asked

"The dreams hurt," I said. "It feels like my guts are on fire."

"Go on."

"In the dreams, I have to go to a VA hospital in Tacoma."

"Tacoma is thirty minutes south of here," she said. "And we do not have a facility there."

"I know, I know. But that's where I go in the dreams, and the white nurses open me up without putting me to sleep."

With renewed interest, she asked, "What does race have to do with it?"

"Oh, I'm sorry. I didn't mean race. There are blue nurses and there are white nurses. Usually the white nurses are nicer than the blue nurses."

"You lost me on that one," she said.

"You know: Some dress in white, some dress in blue."

With a long drawn out okay, she asked, "How long have these dreams gone on?"

"Ever since I was put down here."

"Have you talked to your doctor about this?" she asked.

"He doesn't come to the old folks hospice to visit me," I replied.

"Why do you think this area is a hospice?" she asked.

"Because everyone here is not just older than me, they're ancient. Some look like mummies."

"That's not a nice thing to say."

"I mean it," I said. "I seem to be the only one that gets out of the rooms. Most of them are hooked up to wires that feed the televisions that hang from the ceiling outside our rooms."

"Okay, let's get back to your dreams."

"I keep going back to Tacoma where the nurses open up my gut and I am in great pain. Then I wake up sweating."

"It sounds as if you were given the wrong anesthetic," she said. "I will check into it for you. Now I need to visit some other patients." She left me in the old folks home/hospice waiting area.

Within an hour an orderly pushed a bed down the hallway. It was much longer than the other beds. After a brief pause at the nurses' station, he pushed it into my room. When he came out of my room he was pushing my old small bed. My day had definitely improved.

That evening after dinner, while I was enjoying my new roomy bed, there was a loud crash outside my room. I transferred to my wheelchair to see what had happened. The monitor for the room next to mine had broken loose from the ceiling mount. It lay shattered on the floor squealing. I wheeled out to the nurses' station, a good fifty feet from my room, to report the small disaster where I talked to a rather crude looking fellow who happened to be the union representative for the nurses' union.

"Don't worry about it," he told me. "They'll clean it up first thing in the morning." This guy definitely had job security.

The next morning, fully refreshed after a great night of sleep without any painful dreams, I wheeled out of my room to see an empty bed with a small television and some personal items on top of a bare mattress in place of the shattered monitor from the night before. I had an uneasy feeling as I wheeled past the nurses' station only to hear a night nurse tell an arriving day shift nurse, "We lost Mr. Thompson last night."

The day nurse replied, "Oh, I really liked him."

My monitor still hung precariously outside my room, but at that moment, I was ready to get the hell out of there, metal zipper and all.

That afternoon, just after lunch while I was trying to get comfortable in my long bed, I started experiencing some discomfort with my testicles. They had started to swell. Just as I had achieved more ball room, two effeminate looking doctors arrived in my room. One looked bitch the other butch. One was tall and wore glasses, the other short and squat with a deep voice. They introduced themselves in soft voices as Doctor Dean and Doctor Gene. Great. Dean and Gene, bitch and butch, informed me that they were there to remove the stainless steel staples decorating my gut.

While ignoring me, Dean—or was it Gene—started explaining to bitch or butch how to use the staple puller without taking my skin along with the staples. I am all for diversity in the workplace, but these two guys were off the charts.

After a demonstration removal of one staple, doctor bitch or butch handed the stainless steel high tech staple remover to Dean or Gene and let him at me. I had about thirty or so staples inserted to keep the two halves of my stomach together so it took some time for the trembling hand of Dean or Gene to get them all out.

Free of my stainless steel zipper, I swung my legs onto the floor, stood up and started to lift my backless hospital gown, asking, "Will you guys tell me what's wrong with my balls?"

Both doctors reacted rather more severely than I had expected. Their voices elevated an octave or so yelling, "Stop it," and "No!"

They both came forward and forced me back into my

bed. While they did so, I was able to read their name tags: Nadine and Jean. Both lovely ladies left quickly.

The hospitals in the U S were definitely different than those in Costa Rica.

Later that afternoon, as I was wheeling myself along in my chair through the waiting area of the old folks' home, I saw my vascular surgeon walking past the hallway.

"Doctor Yoshi," I called. "What did you do to my balls?" I was loud enough to get his attention as well as all those in the waiting area.

He rushed over to my wheelchair and asked, in a voice much softer than my outburst, "What seems to be the problem?"

"My balls hurt," I said. "They're really swollen."

"Oh, that sometimes happens to males after an operation," he said. "Any excess fluids will travel to the scrotum. We need to get an ultrasound. I'll arrange it for you. Now, if you will excuse me, I have a bleeder to sew up." And off he went.

The next morning I was sent to the floor where they did X-rays and ultrasound procedures, where I was greeted by the nice lady who had discovered my aneurysm.

"Well, look at you," she said. "All better and raising hell."

"What do you mean?" I responded.

"We all got a chuckle when we heard about you yelling at the good doctor."

"I really am sore and he looked like he was hurrying off, so I sorta yelled to get his attention."

"Well, it worked," she said. "So let's see what's going on, okay? Now, if you will just transfer to the table? Do you need help?"

"Nope," I said, as I locked my wheelchair wheels, stood up and rotated my rear end onto the examination table. Once secure seating was achieved I swung my legs onto the table and lay back.

"Would you please pull up your gown and lower your bottoms?" she said, as she retrieved a tube of jell from a glass of warm water and squirted it onto the wand.

I gave a silent thank you to the ultrasound gods for the warmth of the jell that was about to caress my swollen balls.

The nice lady then proceeded to tickle my testicles with the ultrasound wand for twenty seconds or more until I asked, "Is it too early in our relationship to tell you I think I love you?"

With that remark she dropped the wand and started laughing so hard I thought she would pee her panties. I had surprised myself with the unthinking remark and started laughing also. We carried on with our laughter until a doctor came in and asked us, "What's going on?"

I managed to choke out, "We are in love," before we started up again.

When we had recovered our composure, the invading doctor advised us that another doctor needed to examine my scrotum and I needed to lift it up so that he could keep the boys elevated with a rolled up towel under them. This was accomplished without any mishap. The new doctor came in. She was a young intern, planning on acting professional.

"Wow," I said. "The last time I asked two doctors to look at my testicles, it didn't go too well."

Evidently the story of that incident had made its rounds and all in attendance at my second scrotum party smiled.

COLOR ME HISTORY

After several more days of general mayhem, I was to be discharged into the real world. I spent time visiting all those who had helped me recover from my speed bumps. Abby fitted me with a new wheelchair. As she did so I realized that she would always be a friend, but my true heart belonged to a lost Jackie. Even to this day I think of Abby first amongst the many who gave of their time and expertise to help me.

On the day I was expelled, my son arrived to get me just as the day shift at the hospital was letting out.

As luck and life would have it, Abby and the ultrasound lady were walking out together. I called to them to come over for one last goodbye.

My son stood by as we gave each other wheelchair hugs. The ultrasound Lady said to Abby, "Did I ever tell you what he did to me?"

With that, the two of them started telling stories about many of the stunts I'd been involved with while at the hospital. Abby had the advantage as she had spent the most time with me. She recounted my threats to Beverly when the dog interrupted our walk. I added a few that they didn't know. The anecdotes were all fun and the three of us enjoyed a good laugh while my son listened. It was a brief moment of happiness which made my departure all that more sad. The two ladies asked me kindly not to return. I promised to stay away as long as I lived.

As my son got in the car after stowing my wheelchair in the trunk he said, "You know, dad, someday you should write a book about your time here."

I answered, "You know, son, I might. I just might."

As we drove down the street leading to the highway back to West Seattle, I felt empty. There was a hole where my emotions rested. I was free of the hospital but alone in life. As we swung onto the West Seattle Bridge my son gave me a sideways glance.

"Oh, by the way," he said. "A lady called you from England."

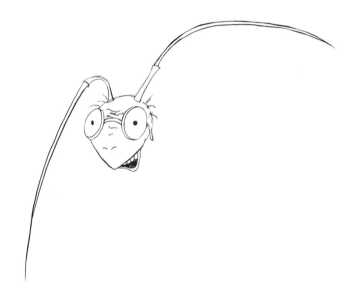

RILEY JACKSON was born in California, lived in Oregon and now resides in Seattle WA. He is living proof that you should pay attention in high school because when he was released from high school he joined the Army during the Korean War. Not one of his brightest moves. He ended up spending most of his three years of active duty in Africa, which is the setting for his next book.

After the service, Riley made his living as a jack of all trades before heading to college for an actual degree. Just a few of the jobs he held include singing, baking donuts, working in a dairy and making pizzas.

Riley graduated from UCSB and accepted his first legitimate job as a systems engineer with RCA systems division. He spent thirty years in the computer industry and marriage. To celebrate the end of those endeavors, he bought a small coffee farm in Costa Rica where this novel starts.

Riley currently lives with the only female in his life, Duchess, a white basset hound. She loves him very much but also drools continuously, sleeps twenty three out of twenty fours a day, and knows more people than Riley does. She is the love of his life and a complete party animal.

ACKNOWLEDGEMENTS

A View from the Floor, was a therapeutic labor of love and survival. The tale begins shortly after my stroke and reflects the paranoia I embraced for several years. My friends were indeed trying to help. It just took a while for me to understand this.

I wish to acknowledge the following people who have provided me with the patience and encouragement that helped me write of my adventure. Chloe, who shared her knowledge and encouragement, and my drinking buddy who shared her Victorian principles and made me tone down some of the more vulgar aspects of my adventure. And finally, my publisher Kristen Morris for her knowledge of the publishing process and superior intellect. She is also stone cold gorgeous.

A special thanks to two individuals whose input took this manuscript from a jumbled mess and turned it into what you read here. Peter Atkins a gifted writer in his own right, who's editing has made me sound literate and Steve Montiglio, a brilliant artist and designer, who happens to have a way with cockroaches in shorts. Thank you both so very much.